T0274365

PRAISE FOR

THE RESET MINDSET

"Not since the Five-Second Rule have I seen a simpler yet more powerful way to change your life!"

MEL ROBBINS

New York Times bestselling author of *The Five-Second Rule* and host of the award-winning *Mel Robbins Podcast*

"*The Reset Mindset* is a transformative guide that adeptly navigates the intersection of personal growth and adaptive change. Zenker's own life experiences lend credence to her powerful methodology, emphasizing the importance of reevaluation and reinvention as vital tools for success in our changing world. This book is an essential read for anyone looking to harness the power of mindset to overcome obstacles and achieve fulfillment, both personally and professionally. With its focus on dynamic reassessment and value creation, *The Reset Mindset* offers practical strategies for those ready to pivot with purpose and embrace the journey of improvement."

DR. MARSHALL GOLDSMITH

Thinkers50 *#1 executive coach and*
New York Times *bestselling author of*
What Got You Here Won't Get You There

"This book embodies the entrepreneurial journey—it's about assessing where you are, rethinking where you're going, and reinventing how you get there. *The Reset Mindset* offers the tools to transform your approach to business and personal goals."

JEFF HOFFMAN

former CEO and cofounder, Priceline.com; coauthor of Scale

"*The Reset Mindset* doesn't just encourage change—it provides a structured approach to ensure that change is both strategic and effective. It's a simple blueprint for those who aim to be right more often than not in a world full of uncertainties."

HOWARD FREIDMAN

CEO, Utz Snacks

"*The Reset Mindset* inspires and guides readers to redirect reflective thinking into high-impact action. Penny Zenker provides clear, specific strategies for both personal and professional development."

DIANNA BOOHER

author of Communicate Like a Leader, Creating Personal Presence, *and* Communicate with Confidence

"*The Reset Mindset* provides actionable insights for anyone looking to approach life with more confidence, clarity, and creativity. Reset your mind with this book."

ROBERT G. ALLEN

#1 New York Times *bestselling author*

"Penny Zenker is a master at cutting through the clutter to help people and organizations supercharge their focus and remain fully aligned on what truly matters. Adopting and implementing *The Reset Mindset* is one of the best decisions you can make."

PAUL EPSTEIN

former NFL and NBA executive; bestselling author of The Power of Playing Offense *and* Better Decisions Faster

"Penny Zenker knocks it out of the park with *The Reset Mindset*. This book is a compelling reminder that resilience, mindfulness, and action are the best ways to own your life and career. This book is a must-read for anyone looking to take their life and leadership to the next level."

KERRY SIGGINS

CEO, StoneAge, and author of The Ownership Mindset

"The concept of Reset Moments was far more contagious than I thought it would be. People have adopted this quickly as a common language in my organization. Building a Reset Mindset in our organization has made a noticeable difference in reducing stress and conflict in the organization and making people more present with options and opportunities."

BRANDON GINSBERG

CEO, ApparelMagic

"The principles of attention management are echoed in this book. Penny's concept of a Reset Mindset is a useful skill for anyone looking to regain control over distraction and be more intentional about achieving their goals. Her framework is simple but powerful, and I recommend adding this book to your library if you're seeking ways to accomplish more of what's most important to you."

MAURA NEVEL THOMAS

productivity expert and author of Attention Management

"*The Reset Mindset* is about more than just thinking differently. It's about implementing real change to achieve your goals. This book is an invaluable resource for anyone pursuing personal and professional excellence."

TONIA JAHSHAN

CEO, Sipology; Canada's #1 female entrepreneur by W100; and Women to Watch on Forbes.com

"In *The Reset Mindset*, leaders will find a brain-friendly blueprint to navigate the chaos and disruption they encounter daily, leading to reduced stress, increased clarity, and enhanced decision-making. I cannot recommend this book highly enough."

DR. JASON JONES

organizational psychologist and bestselling author of Activator

"While *The Reset Mindset* offers a simple yet powerful framework for life change and growth, it is so much more. There are nuggets of wisdom on every page and in every story. It's a motivating read that provides actionable steps that will stay with you."

KEITH ELIAS

senior director of player engagement, NFL

"'There is no more powerful force within our control than the ability to assign meaning' is a profound premise for a book and your life. *The Reset Mindset* will inspire you to transform adversity into your own personal evolution and to enjoy a life rich in meaning and fulfillment."

BRUCE TURKEL

keynote speaker and author of Building Brand Value

"*The Reset Mindset* has so many affirmations of what matters most. One of my favorites is, 'Don't give resources. Help others be more resourceful.' This is true for all leadership roles as well as for teachers."

DONNA GAFFNEY

director of organizational and professional learning at Montgomery County Intermediate Unit

"In a world that never seems to slow down, *The Reset Mindset* is a welcome pause with a powerful message: you have the power to shape your own narratives. With a unique blend of timeless wisdom, current research, and practical advice, it's a must-read for those striving for both personal and professional growth."

NINA NESDOLY

researcher and keynote speaker

"*The Reset Mindset* resonates with the qualities I find essential for success — resilience, strategic execution, and an unwavering commitment to finish what you start. This is a book I would reread over and over again, each time uncovering new layers of wisdom and strategies to apply in my relentless pursuit of excellence. It's a testament to the power of resilience, strategic foresight, and the enduring quest for improvement — a true companion for the journey to achieving lasting success."

STEVEN PIVNIK

bestselling author, advisor, and speaker

"I found myself glued to *The Reset Mindset*. The stories Penny tells are vivid and perfectly aligned with the concepts she is teaching. In my mind, I could see her about to jump out of that airplane! Penny shows we have more control over our situation than we think, and it all has to do with a reset of the mindset."

FRANK BUCK, EdD

author of Get Organized! *and* Get Organized Digitally!

www.amplifypublishinggroup.com

The Reset Mindset: How to Get Unstuck, Focus on What Matters Most, and Reach Your Goals Faster

For more information, please contact:
Amplify Publishing, an imprint of Amplify Publishing Group
620 Herndon Parkway, Suite 220
Herndon, VA 20170
info@amplifypublishing.com

Library of Congress Control Number: 2024904765

CPSIA Code: PRV0424A

ISBN-13: 979-8-89138-229-9

Printed in the United States

To my family and to you, the reader.
May you find the keys to unlocking
your highest potential within these pages.

The
RESET
MINDSET

How to Get Unstuck, Focus on What Matters Most, and Reach Your Goals Faster

PENNY ZENKER

an imprint of Amplify Publishing Group

CONTENTS

INTRODUCTION

FEAR OR EXCITEMENT?

Ten years ago, I found myself soaring ten thousand feet above Las Vegas alongside Lisa, my friend and fellow adventurer. We had paid money to jump out of a perfectly good airplane.

Skydiving had always been on both our bucket lists, so with a nudge from someone in our group, we were booked on this trip. I was trembling with anticipation!

We had gone through the extensive orientation and training—if you want to call five minutes of lying across a stool and being told, "Put your arms out. Don't forget to breathe. Just lift your feet, and you will be fine," *extensive*. The training may have been brief, but the hundred-plus-page waiver was not. Once it was signed, we'd gotten into our flight suits, snapped on our goggles, and met our jump buddies. We were going tandem, which meant we'd each be jumping with an instructor strapped to our backs.

While signing the epic waiver, my excitement had shifted to fear. I quietly wondered, *Was this all the preparation we were going to receive?* Suddenly, instead of eagerly anticipating the rush of the jump, I couldn't help but think about all the things that could go wrong. After all, they were listed right there in black and white. Focus, especially the doomsday variety, has a funny way of amplifying your feelings.

As I walked toward the plane, I got more and more anxious. Even though I had chosen to go skydiving, it seemed scary and daunting now that I was in the heat of the moment. I looked at Lisa. She was obviously nervous, too. As we lined up to board the plane, she pulled me to the back of the line so we could go last. Brilliant plan, right? Put it off for as long as possible.

Proud of ourselves and channeling our nervous energy in another direction, we started to laugh and joke. But as we got to the entrance of the plane, the joke was on us. All the seats were taken. The lead instructor motioned for us to sit on the floor—right in front of the doors.

We went from laughing and joking to crapping our pants as we realized . . . we were going FIRST, not LAST!

They packed us into the plane, and off we went—higher and higher, my fear escalating with the altitude.

My hands were shaking and sweating. My stomach was churning, and my head was spinning. The propellers were loud, like a buzz saw inside my brain. Once we were at altitude, the door abruptly slid open. The gusting wind blew Lisa's long hair straight back, like a flag whipping in a hurricane. I looked down on the clouds and began questioning every decision in my life that had brought me to this point.

The blood drained from Lisa's face as terror took over, and she started to resist the instructor strapped to her back. But he clearly had dealt with this sort of thing before. Implacably, he nudged her forward. As they got to the opening, Lisa grabbed on to the sides of the door. Her knuckles turned white as she tried to hold on for dear life. But the instructor was stronger. He pushed her out, and whooooosh! They were gone.

Over the wind, I could hear Lisa's fear as she screamed her favorite word all the way down: "Fuuuuuuuu . . . !!!"

Suddenly, I felt the instructor pushing me forward. It had become clear that one way or another, I was going to be leaving this plane. I pictured Lisa's face and decided that was not going to be me.

I took what I call a Reset Moment. A purposeful pause. A moment to rethink, reconnect, and be intentional. I needed to reset my mind and body. I took a deep breath and allowed my heart rate to slow, even just a little bit. Then I could take a mental step back and reassess the situation. I remembered that the entire point of doing this was to challenge myself, expand my comfort zone, and experience something new and breathtaking. I could enjoy this ride . . . if I chose to.

So I decided to stop focusing on plummeting to my

death—since that wasn't helping—and chose to shift my focus to the fact that the instructor strapped to me had done this a hundred times before. Literally, he had my back.

With that simple shift in focus, I calmed. Then I plastered a big, fat grin on my face, let go of the urge to resist, and jumped into the blue void.

That feeling of flight was unforgettable. Seeing the world from this incredible viewpoint made me feel so present and alive. I can't explain it; it shifted something in me. Seeing the Earth from ten thousand feet changes the way you look at your whole life.

When I reached the ground, Lisa was already there, still pale and shaking. Even though we had both just taken the same wild ride, we'd each had a very different experiences.

By taking a moment to reset and take back control of my skydiving experience, I didn't get pushed, like Lisa did.

I jumped.

That is the power of the Reset Mindset.

The Reset Mindset makes you more conscious of your choices, purposeful in your actions, and targeted toward results.

CHAPTER 1

WHAT IS THE RESET MINDSET?

The Reset Mindset has been a part of my life in some shape or form since I was nineteen years old, when my father died in a tragic accident (more on that later in the book). Resetting began simply as a coping mechanism—a way to self-regulate and put me back in control at a time when I was feeling that my life was totally out of control.

During this period, resetting was so effective that I eventually asked myself—*Why wait for the big, life-changing moments to come along when it is possible to realign my thinking and reset my focus at any time?* So I started looking for more and more opportunities—Reset Moments—to take a step forward by taking a step back.

Life can be messy, complex, and uncertain. A Reset Mindset ultimately helped me make the complex simple, and I truly believe this has been the driver of my successes and personal fulfillment. It can be yours too.

Disruption and change are the only constants in today's business environment. As a result, mindset in the workplace has come to be seen as a vital component of organizational culture and performance across all industries. Mindset is recognized as a driver of innovation, productivity, and adaptability—qualities that are crucial for success in today's fast-paced and ever-changing business environment.

Much of this recognition started in 2006 when Carol Dweck opened up the conversation about how mindset influences personal and professional success in her book *Mindset: The New Psychology of Success.* Her groundbreaking work draws a distinction between a Fixed Mindset and a Growth Mindset, and shows the power of the Growth Mindset.

The impact on business culture is measurable. Studies have shown that employees in growth-minded environments are 34 percent more likely to feel a strong sense of commitment to the company and 47 percent more likely to say that their colleagues are trustworthy.*

---

*HBR editors. "How Companies Can Profit from a 'Growth Mindset.'" *Harvard Business Review*, November 2014. https://hbr.org/2014/11/how-companies-can-profit-from-a-growth-mindset.

Organizations like NixonMcInnes have implemented practices that specifically foster a Growth Mindset, such as their "Church of Fail" gatherings where employees openly discuss their professional failures and explore alternative strategies, thereby creating a culture of learning and evolution.

The United States Navy is another example. They have adopted a mindset model known as "Get Real, Get Better," which is designed to promote a culture of continuous improvement and learning. This approach encourages sailors and officers to face challenges and failures head-on, assess them honestly (getting real), and use them as opportunities for growth and improvement (getting better).

Before we dive into the Reset Mindset and how it is different from others, let's define mindset to share a common understanding.

A mindset is a way of thinking, a mental filter that colors what we see and how we think about the world. It steers our attention to certain things and shapes our reactions to what happens to us and around us. Now let's define a Reset Mindset and compare it to the Growth Mindset for reference.

A Growth Mindset is a belief that we can improve our abilities and intelligence through practice, effort, and learning from our mistakes. A person with a Growth

Mindset views challenges and obstacles as opportunities, and believes failure is just a temporary setback that one can learn from. It's about embracing challenges, persisting in the face of setbacks, learning from experience, and finding inspiration in others' successes.

A Reset Mindset is a way of thinking that focuses on dynamic reassessment and the willingness to reinvent.

Both the Growth Mindset and the Reset Mindset are grounded in maximizing potential and turning challenges into opportunities, but they are built on a different foundation. A Growth Mindset is grounded in learning to adapt to change, and a Reset Mindset is grounded in value creation to create change. The Reset Mindset is about proactively driving change, reframing setbacks for a new focus, reassessing a complex problem, or making new connections to leverage a new opportunity. You are constantly reevaluating your current goals and priorities to ensure your focus and energy are aligned with your values and greater aspirations. In doing so, you renew your sense of purpose and strategy.

While a Growth Mindset focuses on evolving within the path you're currently on, a Reset Mindset focuses on a willingness to change the path itself to iteratively adapt to new information or circumstances as you go. The distinction is crucial because they each have unique impacts on how

A Reset Mindset is a way of thinking that focuses on dynamic reassessment and the willingness to reinvent.

individuals and organizations approach development and change. The chart on the next page outlines the differences in focus between the mindset types.

Both the Growth and Reset approaches agree that there is no finish line. There can always be further improvement or adaptation to changing circumstances. However, a Reset Mindset can provide a competitive advantage by enabling quicker adaptation to industry trends and disruptions, potentially outpacing competitors.

And it may not just be a matter of competitive advantage—it may even be a matter of survival. Back in 1849, Charles Darwin wrote a universal truth. "It is not the most intellectual of the species that survives. It is not the strongest that survives. The species that survives is the

	FIXED MINDSET	GROWTH MINDSET	RESET MINDSET
GROWTH	Limited view of potential	Learning to reach potential	Focus on value creation
ABILITIES	Views abilities as unchangeable	Developing abilities through effort	Quick adapt to change
SETBACKS	Avoids challenges, threatened by failures	Learning from failures, viewing challenges as opportunities	Reframing setbacks for new focus
TIME FOCUS	Resistance to change	Long-term development	Short-term agility
VALUES	Innate talent	Effort and progress	Feedback and agility
LEARNING	Stick to what they know	Embraces learning from experience	Contextual learning
RESILIENCE	Gives up easily, lacks resilience	Resilience through learning	Dynamic reassessment
IMPROVEMENT	Status quo mentality	Incremental improvements	Willingness to reinvent
FEEDBACK	Defensive	Desired and periodic	Required and frequent
ROLE OF THE PAST	Holds onto past failures and successes	Views past as a learning opportunity	Uses past to redefine future

one that is able best to adapt and adjust to the changing environment in which it finds itself."

For example, Nokia was the leading mobile phone vendor in the world until early 2011. Due to its slow adaptation to newer smartphone technologies, they gradually lost market share and sold to Microsoft in 2013. At the end of his speech during the sale, the CEO said, "We didn't do anything wrong, but somehow we lost." They lost because they didn't adapt quickly enough to the changing environment, and they were not willing to reinvent themselves.

We know that personal growth and transformation are possible because the human brain has a remarkable capacity to change and adapt. The Reset Mindset is firmly built on the concept of neuroplasticity—our brain's proven ability to reorganize itself and form new neural connections.

In neuropsychologist Donald Hebb's book *The Organization of Behavior*, he wrote, "Neurons that fire together wire together" to describe how pathways in the brain are formed and reinforced through repetition. In other words, our brain clusters our beliefs to make implementing them more efficient. It's much like the operating system on your computer. Your reactions "load" automatically, like software. But because it takes programming to achieve these clusters, you can influence your mindset by choosing which actions and behaviors you want to perform repeatedly.

Or think of it as muscle memory—like a pianist's fingers that glide over the keys after repeating the same music that has been practiced over and over, or a speed cuber that runs through well-practiced algorithms to solve the Rubik's Cube in a matter of seconds, or even simply riding a bike or tying your shoes. By engaging in consistent repetition, the tasks that once demanded conscious attention eventually become second nature.

The same process applies to your thought patterns when facing change, challenges, or uncertainty. With each repeated mental shift, your brain becomes more proficient at adapting, reassessing, and reframing your thoughts. This practiced flexibility becomes automatic, allowing you to tap into creativity and effortlessly assess relevancy, value, and priorities. Over time, just as muscles remember movements, our brains remember this adaptive way of thinking, making it an instinctive part of how we confront new situations.

While it's true that much of your mindset has been programmed by your upbringing and ingrained biases and assumptions, you have the capability to reprogram it! You can *choose* which thoughts, actions, and behaviors you want to perform repeatedly.

Once you activate your Reset Mindset, you will automatically reassess the way you approach people, problems, and opportunities. You will be able to reinvent (and reprogram!) yourself again and again. As circumstances change, you can adapt so that your business does not fall behind. You'll be able to accept that the best practices of yesterday may not be the best practices for today, much less tomorrow. And you'll welcome change instead of fearing it, because you are always willing to look honestly and objectively at what's working and what's not.

Repetition is the key to learning, and I want the Reset Mindset to stick with you long after you read this book. It's all about conditioning. The conditioning—the muscle memory and repetition—that builds your Reset Mindset is found in the Reset Practice.

The Reset Practice rewires your brain to create a Reset Mindset.

The Reset Practice has three simple steps. The simplicity is intentional so that you can access these steps not only in the good and easy times but, even more importantly, in the challenging and uncertain ones. Maybe you remember the simple steps of extinguishing a fire: stop, drop, and roll. We need simple practices to fall back on during stressful times. Simplicity is the antidote to complexity.

The three steps of the Reset Practice are:

1. Step Back
2. Get Perspective
3. Realign

In the coming chapters, we will dive deeper into each of these three steps, how they can be enacted in your life, how they can be an integral part of your leadership, and how to use them to support the development of other leaders.

Reset Moments can be big (like jumping out of a plane) or small, like taking a five-minute break between meetings or a deep breath before you speak during a

Simplicity is the antidote to complexity.

heated discussion. But whatever its size and duration, each and every one of them has the chance to positively impact your life. They can turn ordinary moments into moments that matter. This is because Reset Moments are conscious choice points—a structured space to rethink, reconnect, and realign with what matters most.

As seen in the chart on the following page, this dynamic reassessment is a critical feedback loop to ensure that growth is not only sustained but also optimized in alignment with the ever-evolving external environment.

Obviously, if you miss the signs to reset, no change happens. Recognizing a Reset Moment when it presents itself intuitively activates the Reset Practice, which is the *how-to* that results in maximizing your potential regardless of the

Reset Moments can turn ordinary moments into moments that matter.

circumstances. And with enough consistent practice, you will build *your* Reset Mindset. Mine is now innate, my default setting. It helps me leave the ego behind. It creates the emotional balance to see things as they truly are, so I can focus on the right things and make purposeful, informed, effective decisions.

There will be several tools that directly support this practice. Some may be familiar, while others may be new to you. Either way, remember, it isn't enough merely to know about these tools. You have to consistently practice them.

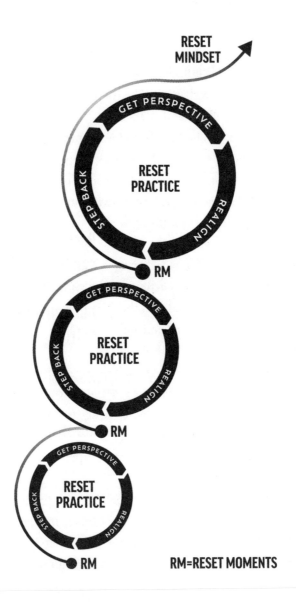

RESET MINDSET

GET PERSPECTIVE

RESET PRACTICE

STEP BACK

REALIGN

RM

GET PERSPECTIVE

RESET PRACTICE

STEP BACK

REALIGN

RM

GET PERSPECTIVE

RESET PRACTICE

STEP BACK

REALIGN

RM

RM=RESET MOMENTS

Every business leader I talk to wants to grow their company and business exponentially, but they often get lost along the way. It does not matter if you are a corporate CEO, a manager in a Fortune 500 company, an entrepreneur building your business from the ground up, or a work-at-home mom or dad.

Building a Reset Mindset will empower you to streamline your business structure, identify key issues, reevaluate operations, examine core functions, and distinguish what procedures and processes are no longer serving your company.

Reset Moments are conscious choice points—a structured space to rethink, reconnect, and realign with what matters most.

Whether you are innovating, optimizing, operating, or selling, the Reset Mindset will give you a decisive competitive advantage. It is equal parts performance, leadership, and resilience strategies all rolled into one.

All of that is possible with this simple, three-step practice.

Even if you do intend to apply this concept primarily to your business, over time you may find that this new way of thinking impacts far more. You wear many other hats, too: leader, partner, parent, friend, colleague. The practice of resetting is more than just a leadership strategy. It shapes your internal dialogue, which impacts every decision you make and how you approach every challenge—professional and personal. As the saying goes, how we do something is how we do everything.

Allow yourself a moment for honest and objective self-assessment.

Are you ready to institutionalize this way of thinking, to empower your teams and organization? Do you want to create a standard that facilitates and accelerates growth and development in your organization and your life? When was the last time you honestly assessed your leadership and the results you are currently getting?

We all want meaningful results to define our success and align with our values, but this doesn't happen magically.

It happens one Reset Moment at a time.

No Going Back

Burnout, quiet quitting, change fatigue—call it whatever you want. We (and by *we*, I mean *all of us*) are exhausted and distracted, critical and hesitant. We feel out of control. How did we get here?

Markets and behaviors are constantly changing. As a result, communication gets more and more scattered and unclear. Information may be abundant, but insights are rare, priorities are blurred, and leadership is scrambling. We want to focus on the right things, but I have found through my audience surveys and private clients that the single biggest stressor reported is competing priorities. It shouldn't be a surprise that when we make everything urgent and important, nothing is. Universal urgency becomes another agent of distraction. Competing priorities are a core driver of stress. They lead to overload and overwhelm.

This lack of clarity leaves people feeling overwhelmed, unappreciated, and skeptical of leadership. Trust melts under the heat of those pressures. As people disengage and become more complacent and apathetic, their collaboration decreases, their creativity drops, and their productivity declines.

We cannot go back to business as usual. Even if we could, why would we want to? Would that really solve our problems? The truth is, these problems aren't new; they were just amplified by the COVID-19 pandemic. We are in the midst of a massive, shared Reset Moment. As markets, people, and circumstances change, so must we. If we're aiming for a workplace where clarity reigns, creativity thrives, and adaptability is second nature, then we need better strategies to navigate change and build resilience into the bones of our business culture. Better technology or more-efficient processes will only take you so far. It's how we adapt to our ever-changing environment, how we rethink team dynamics, and how we work together that will drive our future success.

Once you view your job and relationships through a Reset Mindset, nothing will ever be the same. You will feel grounded and in control, even in times of great change, challenge, and uncertainty. You will reconnect to your creativity and passion, perhaps long dormant or feared lost, and be able to maintain your focus, whatever the circumstances.

The Reset Mindset doesn't require financial investment or hours of training. You can continuously build and strengthen it, wherever and whenever you want.

You already instinctively understand it, and you may even be doing it from time to time in some shape or form. But there is a gap between *knowing* and *doing*. And a gap between *occasionally* and *consistently*.

Let's close those gaps.

From Why to What to How

One night, in my sophomore year at Drexel, I had just returned from class. I was hungry and needed to unwind, so I ordered a pizza. A few minutes later, the buzzer rang, but instead of the pizza delivery person, my older brother stood there. I was confused. My brother lived an hour away.

Why was he standing at my door?

Then he spoke the worst words I could have imagined: "Penny, there was an accident. Dad died."

I screamed so hard the windows shook. I was sobbing, and my brother held me as he told me what had happened. My father, at the age of fifty-eight, had received a glancing blow from a bus. After stumbling forward, he'd fallen and hit his head on the curb. If he had fallen from any other angle, he might have simply broken an arm or a leg, but he fell on the precise spot that instantly rendered him brain-dead. I was shattered. I cried until everything faded away. I went completely numb. It had never crossed my mind that someone I loved might die so suddenly. For the first time, I was exposed to the harsh reality that we can't plan or choose everything that happens in life.

We cannot go back to business as usual.

In the following weeks, I broke up with my boyfriend, moved home, and isolated myself from everyone. Why? I have no idea. It was instinctive. I felt like everything was unraveling, and taking extreme action was the only thing I could control. I've since learned that most people take drastic action when under severe stress, pressure, or uncertainty. Those actions are a way of asserting control when we feel like we have none.

For six months, I felt alone and sorry for myself, and I kept asking, *Why?* over and over, but answers never came. Impulsively, I took a semester abroad. I had to get away, get outside my everyday environment, find a new perspective, and look at things with fresh eyes.

I won't lie. It was hard. I didn't know anyone. And frankly, I didn't want to get to know anyone, either. I felt hopelessly alone and out of place. But often, it is only by going far away that we are able to find what was right in front of us. It can be easier to see what is holding us back when we detach from our day-to-day environment. So the distance and the discomfort did their work, and eventually I made a discovery.

My discovery wasn't intellectual or academic. It was humanistic and visceral. I stopped asking why. Because clearly, this question had no answer, and even if there were an answer, it wouldn't bring my dad back or change the situation. Under the right context, *Why?* can be a powerful connection to something greater. But in this circumstance, asking the question was an emotional trap holding me back from accepting the situation and moving through my grief. *Why?* had become the rabbit I chased but could never catch.

Something shifted, and I began instead to ask what I found to be a far more impactful question: *What does this mean?*

What does this mean? is the unconscious question we ask ourselves in every situation and circumstance, every moment of every day. And there is no more powerful force within our control than the ability to assign meaning.

When we bring this question into our consciousness and apply a spirit of true curiosity, it enables us to control the meaning of all of life's experiences—even those that often seem meaningless or random like my dad's death. It's powerful because the same event or interaction may have a different meaning for you than for me. It's powerful because the idea of *meaning* and the act of seeking it can be multilayered and various—and can be literal or metaphorical.

This shift in my perspective from *Why?* to *What does this mean?* was my first experience of the power of the Reset Mindset. And as my perspective shifted, I began to notice comparable shifts in my attitudes, expectations, and priorities.

What does this mean? was no mere "research" tool. Sure, there may be objective, inherent meaning in things, but asking the question also opened up opportunities for perspective-taking and choosing. With this question, I created a conscious choice about what this life-changing event could mean.

There is no more powerful force within our control than the ability to assign meaning.

This newfound power to choose meaning revealed even more contours to the Reset Mindset. Not only can the same singular event have different meanings for you than for me, but that one event can also contain multiple meanings for each of us.

Reflecting and reassessing allows you to continuously find new meanings in an event, evolving the question from *What does this mean?* to *What ELSE could this mean?* And *What ELSE?* And *What ELSE?*

Why ask again and again? Because the first answer is almost never the strongest answer. My first answer might be my preprogrammed answer from my ego, fears, or biases, but it's not necessarily the best answer. Digging deeper with greater curiosity is how to gain perspective.

This question opened up even more options, which allowed me to make even better choices. This question empowered me to *assign* meaning.

Look at something as commonplace as another driver cutting you off in traffic. They could just be a horrible and selfish human being, sure. But . . . *What else could this mean?* Maybe they are late for work or got an emergency call from a loved one. Maybe they're from out of town and don't know the traffic patterns. Maybe they themselves were just cut off and are going through their own emotional reaction to that mighty injustice!

When you choose to understand there are LOTS of potential correct answers . . . you are freed. You are free to choose the correct answer with the most empowering meaning. This is important because the meaning you give a situation is how you see, think, and feel about the situation. That will impact how you interact with it, and ultimately, the results you get.

Initially, the question *What does this mean?* allowed me to see that the right answer wasn't to hold someone accountable or get lost in blame. Choosing that meaning would only fill me with more anger and extend my grieving. The right answer for me was to use this tragedy to deepen my relationships, give myself greater purpose, and live my best life. Through the process of healing, I deepened my self-awareness, and reclaimed my self-confidence.

I could have given this a meaning that life is hard, don't trust others, don't take risks, and live an overprotected life with an undertone of fear. But I chose the opposite. I chose to see that life is NOW. We don't know what tomorrow brings. Try new things. Take chances. Explore. Love. Forgive.

That was probably the greatest gift I received from my father's death. I learned how to assign meaning from a young age in a way that empowers me.

Today, I continue to empower myself to make big choices. But when I fall now, I apply the power of asking *What else could this mean?* and choose a meaning that allows me to keep pushing to reach my true potential. Consider how basic and simple this power is. It's not just about cause and effect. We cannot author facts, but we can author their interpretation and relevance. We can choose the path of empowerment rather than the path of victimization. Having experienced the ultimate example—my father's far-too-early death—I came to understand that while we have no control over what time we have, we have complete control over what we choose to focus on.

This simple question—*What ELSE could this mean?*—has profound organizational value, too. Asking the question multiple times reflects the very nature of the Reset Mindset, which is based on reassessing, probing, and challenging.

There were two major influences that shaped my Reset Mindset at work.

First, I read Tim Ferriss's first book, *The 4-Hour Workweek*, but I was not impressed. It seemed like a book of shortcuts and hacks. At the time, I was working around the clock in my technology business and discounted his ideas as impossible or impractical. It wasn't until years later that I saw the deeper meaning in his way of thinking. Tim was struggling with burnout himself, and set himself a constraint

The Reset Mindset is based on reassessing, probing, and challenging.

of working four hours a week to create a lifestyle business. He could no longer run his business the same way, so he had to transform the way he worked, and the constraints he set became his catalyst for creativity. I had been so focused on what he was *doing*, but the real gold for me was in the way he was *thinking*.

When I finally understood the power of constraints, I leveraged the question *What else does this mean?* into *How else can I approach this?* And *HOW ELSE?* Because the more you ask *How else?*, the more lateral your thinking becomes.

A few years later, while running a division for GfK, I came across *Blue Ocean Strategy* by Chan Kim and Renée Mauborgne. The Blue Ocean Strategy involves repeatedly asking *How else?* to uncover creative and innovative ideas. This approach encourages continuous questioning and rethinking of traditional business models and strategies. By persistently exploring alternative perspectives and possibilities, you challenge the status quo, leading to the discovery of untapped markets, or "Blue Oceans." These markets are free from fierce competition, allowing for the creation of unique value propositions and capturing new demand. Essentially, it's about breaking away from the "Red Oceans" of intense competition by repeatedly questioning and innovating until a novel, uncontested market space is identified.

In each of these constructs, we can see how not settling for the first answer, but digging deeper and asking better questions directs our ability to adapt, optimize, and innovate.

When you adopt these questions collectively as a tool, you redefine your corporate culture. You move away from assigning fault and toward empowering each other—from questioning your circumstances to defining your responses and opportunities. This shift in perspective is a powerful antidote to toxicity. It breeds a culture rich in collaboration, resilience, and authentic connection.

Stop the Tug of War

The subtitle of my first book, *The Productivity Zone*, was *Stop the Tug of War with Time*. The tension is between the demands on our time and the amount of time actually available to us. The pandemic revealed to me that this concept extends far beyond what I initially imagined.

We don't just have a tug-of-war with time but also with our health, our relationships, our finances, and even our values and principles. The official definition of "tug-of-war" is a *struggle for control*. After further thought and research, I concluded that the struggle for control is our greatest source of conflict and stress.

Every day, we deplete our energy by getting angry, wasting time, and exhausting ourselves trying to control everything and everyone around us. In 2019, the World Health Organization declared stress the health epidemic of the twenty-first century. According to a 2020 American Psychological Association survey, the problem

The struggle for control is our greatest source of conflict and stress.

is getting worse. Our bodies and minds are suffering from compounding stressors, and we are chronically in a fight-or-flight response. By 2022, 77 percent of employees had experienced burnout symptoms (Deloitte). And when people feel helpless and overwhelmed, they strive to gain control by any means necessary, even if those means are unhealthy or harmful. We know this is true because we have probably all experienced this at some point in our lives.

Physiologically and biologically, the impulse to control is a self-preservation mechanism. This need can spike and create the so-called "control freaks" within us, like your micromanagers, nitpickers, and naysayers. But evolutionarily speaking, the need for control is ultimately just about our core human needs for stability, comfort, and reassurance.

But the growing global trends in market instability, anxiety, loneliness, and depression are exacerbating the negative side of these control needs, resulting in a zero-sum, "control or be controlled" mindset. This control-or-be-controlled mentality is a trap because focusing on things we can't actually control leaves us drained, overwhelmed, and too exhausted to address the things we actually can. Ultimately, we give up our power and agency, ensuring that the tug-of-war never ends.

What if . . . we simply let go of the rope? Because try as we might, we cannot control external forces. But we can control how we respond to them. Bestselling author and expert on grief Brian Kessler wrote, "The closest to being in control we'll ever be is in that moment when we realize we're not." It may seem counterintuitive at first, but only by accepting that we cannot control everything—and then letting go of what is beyond our control—can we begin to focus our energy and effort on those things that we can.

We Are Creatures Who Feel

It had been one of those rough mornings. The kids weren't listening. It had taken forever to get them in the car and buckled up. Traffic was a mess. I was already late for work, and as I was speeding to daycare, my son and daughter started fighting in the back seat. I buckled under the stress and shouted at my son. He screamed back, and our screaming match escalated. After I dropped him off, I felt so awful I had to pull over. "What just happened?" I asked myself. "Who was that?" My reaction to the situation was not how I wanted to show up as a mother, and I felt deeply ashamed of how I had behaved.

There, idling at the curb, feeling regretful, I took a Reset Moment. I accepted that stress had overwhelmed me, that I had lost control and reacted with anger. I vowed next time a similar moment arose (whether with my son, my daughter, a coworker, or really anyone I crossed paths with), I would have a better strategy to maintain control and be the kind of mother, friend, colleague, and person I wanted to be.

I had a choice. Instead of continuing to beat myself up (which I often did), I reminded myself that I am human. You are too. This is also something we must constantly remind ourselves about our leaders. All leaders, first and foremost, are *people,* and therefore, they are subject to being driven by their emotions. Humans are not thinking creatures who feel; they are feeling creatures who think. Rather than trying to manage emotions as they happen, choose simple preventive methods to avoid emotional triggers and de-escalate the situation quickly. The sooner we recognize the Reset Moment, the more likely we are to proactively avoid an unproductive confrontation.

For example, with my kids, I found it effective to use Thomas W. Phelan's 1-2-3 Magic method. With this method, when your child talks back to you (for example), you say, "That's one." They do it again, you say, "That's two." etc. If the warning is not heeded by your child, you give them the space to calm down by calling a time-out. Having a predetermined way to handle a situation removed the stress and emotion by detaching me from taking the confrontation personally.

I also have a method for de-escalation in the heat of an argument. I borrow a simple phrase from *Parenting with*

Building a Reset Mindset will give you a mechanism to accept that control over external factors is nothing but an illusion.

Love and Logic, by Foster Cline and Jim Fay. When I'm approaching that place where I know I'm about to say something I'll regret, I respond with, "I love you too much to argue." This statement reduces the intensity of the moment, aligns me with my intentions, and immediately stops that tug of war.

Similarly, at work, to avoid escalation or blind spots, I ask myself, "What expectation isn't being met?" or "What am I missing?" By asking myself those questions, I remind myself to exercise curiosity rather than reacting defensively. From a curious state, I'm able to ask clarifying questions. Without a clear understanding of expectations, conflict is inevitable, because mismatched expectations drive people's frustration.

It isn't personal. It's personality.

I also like to say, "It isn't personal. It's personality." Because conflict is usually more of a matter of differing personalities and styles in handling a situation than it is true animosity or antagonism.

It isn't about scripting a way to deal with conflict, because I can't know what you actually are going to say or do. Your way of dealing with conflict might be different than mine. It's simply about having a phrase or question to remind you what's important, so you can reframe your mental and emotional states. That way, no matter the difficulty of the moment, you can be effective.

Whether it is parenting, interacting with a spouse, or dealing with a colleague at work, the practice is the same. Reset Practices help us *detach* from taking situations personally, *unpack* what we are feeling, and *make better decisions* in the midst of emotionally charged moments.

Reset Practices help us *detach* from taking situations personally, *unpack* what we are feeling, and *make better decisions* in the midst of emotionally charged moments.

Make the Complex Simple

After four years of running a technology company that I built from just me to a multimillion-dollar enterprise, I may have looked to many people like a real success.

But the truth was much harsher. My business was killing me. I was working incredibly hard, but I was not working smart. At all.

Instead of taking the time (the Reset Moments!) to think through problems, I'd throw money at them. But of course, that didn't solve them. In fact, that approach usually cost me more time and money than it saved.

I had zero boundaries. I said yes to every opportunity, regardless of capacity or fit. As a result, I worked nights, holidays, and weekends. I had this little voice in my head that would say, "Penny, just work a few more hours, and you'll catch up or get it all done." I should've known better, but I followed that voice's horrible advice anyway, just to make it go away. I had neither the solutions to my self-made predicament nor the time to think of any.

To make matters worse, I was also a terrible micro-manager. Because the business was growing so fast (yes, a good problem), I felt out of control. So I tried to control everything and everyone.

Even when I *did* manage to delegate something to someone else, I would then hover over their shoulder, telling them exactly how to do the task or just taking it back and doing it myself. But by taking those tasks away, I fell right into the trap of the accountability paradox. Because I subverted the autonomy of my team, they became disengaged, which made them feel less ownership over their work and, therefore, less inspired to be held accountable.

The result of all this dysfunction stacking on itself? I was *burned out*.

So when I had the opportunity to sell my business, I jumped at it. The grass has got to be greener over there, right? I told myself I could make this move and get away from all the stress and overwhelm I was mired in.

That's when I met Peter, GfK Switzerland's board chairman and my new boss (and, ultimately, a treasured mentor). And I thought, THIS IS IT! This is my nine-to-five dream job. A big corporation with deep pockets and an abundance of resources. All my problems would disappear.

Following a thorough interview with Peter, I was hired as Chief Technology Officer of a daughter company of one of the world's largest marketing companies. During that interview, sitting in Peter's plush office, I imagined what it would be like to have extensive company resources and support systems. No more shoestring budgets, twenty-four-hour workdays, or limited staff! I couldn't wait to start.

But then, in my first week, Peter asked me to take part in

a special task force to reorganize the company, because the subsidiary was underperforming. And then he offered me the CEO position of the organization's holding company, making me responsible for five group companies in four countries.

Um. Whoa. Hold on a second. This was not what I had signed up for!

The magnitude of my new role in St. Gallen, a remote town in Switzerland, made me feel like an imposter before I even began. It wasn't the leisurely ride I had imagined. I remember thinking, "Penny, you don't have the experience for this. You don't even know the language. There's no way you'll be able to do this job." My excitement cratered. My self-confidence dove to an all-time low.

To make matters worse, due to the restructuring, I had to lay off forty people *on my first day*. I felt sick, anxious, and overwhelmed as I stood in front of all employees to deliver the bad news.

As I began my speech, I started in German, intending to say something clever to bridge the language gap before switching to English. I meant to say, "My German is rusty" ("Mein Deutsch ist Hartzig"), but instead, I said, "Mein Deutsch is Hertzig," which means "My German is cute." If you're reminded of John F. Kennedy in West Berlin trying to say "Ich bin Berliner" and accidentally saying "Ich bin ein Berliner," which translates to "I am a jelly doughnut," you're not wrong.

My blunder may not have been televised, but I was still mortified. Even with my mediocre German, I could understand what the employees were whispering to each other: "How can she lead the company if she can't even speak German?" Determined to make it work, that was the last day I spoke English in the office. It was German, and German only, from that day forward.

My first few months were chaotic as I got to know the organization, its processes, and its people. But no matter how hard I tried, I felt like I was sinking in the deep end. Just as I put out one fire, another would blaze up. It was one major project after another, with no time to get up to speed.

"Hey, Penny, our software company in India is about to make a major new release, but testing is unsuccessful. What should we do?"

"Hey, Penny, the Austrian group needs a new CEO. Who should we hire?"

"Hey, Penny, one of our suppliers is late in delivery, how do we manage the customer?"

Hey, Penny. Hey, Penny. Hey, Penny.

Then I received a critical thirty-page client contract. In German. And I had less than twenty-four hours to review it. The contract contained significant risk. Could we deliver? Would we damage our reputation? We can't control other suppliers! Was it even an option not to take it?

Bang. I hit my breaking point. I set up a meeting with Peter. I entered his office, where so recently I had dreamed of my perfect new job. I didn't want to let Peter down, but at the same time, I couldn't go on.

My heart was pounding. I took a deep breath. My voice cracked as I said, "I quit."

Peter remained silent as I nervously explained my trials and tribulations. His silence was unnerving, but I persisted.

"I have never managed this many people, directly or indirectly, let alone through a turnaround. I just finished four years of working ungodly hours, and this is NOT what I signed up for."

Silence. Nothing. Not a word.

Peter listened quietly from behind his oversized oak desk overlooking Lake Lucerne until I got everything off my chest. After a long silence, he finally said, "I understand you feel overwhelmed now. I watched you closely during the hiring process and the task-force evaluation. I saw how purposefully you approached the process, your focus on what was important, and your ability to identify and solve problems. I am confident you are the right person for this role. Penny, I hired you to make decisions. What you do with the rest of your time is up to you."

What you do with the rest of your time is up to you?

$$\circlearrowleft \quad \cdot$$

At first, this overly simplistic statement frustrated me. As did Peter's refusal to just tell me what to do. But the more I thought about it, the more I realized Peter was right. Peter had thrown me into the deep end—team layoffs, language barriers, the high-risk contract—precisely because he believed in my strong decision-making.

After so many years of being intimately hands-on with every aspect of my own business, letting go of control was a challenge. I could not be involved in that level of detail and stay focused on the bigger objectives of my role. I had to let go, not only so others could fully own their responsibilities but also so I could fully own mine.

Peter also understood that telling me what to do would not empower my leadership. It would not instill ownership of the problem. His response forced me to step back and think for myself, reconnect to the objective, and make my own decisions about the best ways to refocus on the right things.

Peter taught me with this simple statement that people usually don't need resources—they need resourcefulness.

People usually don't need resources— they need resourcefulness.

Like many people transitioning into new positions or operating under high stress with competing priorities, I had lost control of my focus. I thought I could increase output simply by pouring more and more time into *doing* instead of *deciding*. It's a tempting false premise: more time spent equals greater output. But that idea is simply not true. Productivity is not determined by time spent but by speed to impact.

It seems crazy that a simple quote or statement can shift our whole outlook, but it can. Its simplicity can give us clarity and makes it stick. I reflected further on Peter's statement. My responsibilities hadn't changed. My circumstances hadn't changed. But with that shift in perspective, my responses—both emotional and intellectual—completely changed.

I didn't quit. Now that I looked at my circumstances differently, I could approach them differently. And I thrived.

Peter's advice is now firmly entrenched in my Reset Mindset.

Productivity is not determined by time spent but by speed to impact.

Own Your Focus

This concept has value far beyond work. Every aspect of our modern life is assaulted by distraction. Building and maintaining your Reset Mindset can help you *own your focus.*

Today, focus is the exception, not the rule. We swipe, scroll, tap, and touch our phones *three thousand times each day.* When our phone dings with a notification, whether from a text, social media post, or email, our average response time is *ninety seconds.** How many notifications do you receive in a day? How can we focus when we are incessantly bombarded by distractions, never mind the bigger picture of constant changes in the marketplace?

* Worldwide Texting Statistics, https://shso.vermont.gov/sites/ghsp/files/documents/Worldwide%20Texting%20Statistics.pdf.

And our unrealistic need to respond immediately to every little notification has created an environment overflowing with false urgencies and impossible expectations. According to NordVPN, fully two-thirds of adults today even use their phones *in the bathroom*. What started out as a productivity tool has turned into a weapon of mass distraction. (Full disclosure: I even once had the almost uncontrollable impulse to grab my phone during a funeral for my dear aunt Arlene. What could possibly have been so important?)

Distraction is like sugar: the more we are distracted, the more we want to be distracted—to the point we literally become addicted. This is no mere theory. It's chemical. Many types of modern distractions trigger the reward center in our brains and release dopamine, similar to drug addictions. And the more distracted we are, the more we feel out of control, and the less we own our focus.

There's a simple solution, even to something as insidious as distraction. I bet you know what I'm going to say. Yep. The Reset Mindset. Reset Moments act as a centering strategy, like meditation, bringing your attention back to the present and to what matters most, reconnecting you to higher objectives. Your Reset Practices help you plan for and block out distraction.

Reset Moments keep you aware, objective, and adaptable, whatever the situation. Like anything, mastery requires repetition. With enough repetition, you will find yourself making and taking more Reset Moments instinctively, without even thinking about it, because that's how our brains work. Think about the wonder of the Reticular Activating System (RAS), which is a network of neurons in our brain stem. The RAS regulates arousal, consciousness, and motivation. Basically, it's a filter. The amount of stimulus and sensory input assailing the brain at any moment is overwhelming. The RAS, because it sits between the senses and the brain, guards the brain from overload by filtering out what's important and what can be ignored. That's right—your brain purposely ignores huge amounts of information by distorting, distracting, and generalizing. Otherwise, it wouldn't be able to function. The RAS lets in what's essential while tuning out what's unnecessary. Like a bouncer at the velvet rope of your brain.

By taking advantage of what's already hardwired into us, we can hack our brains. Think about the first few times you tried to tie your shoes when you were a kid. It took all your concentration. Same with learning to drive a car. It's nerve-racking at first, but then driving becomes second nature because your brain has been trained. The RAS knows what to let in and what to keep out.

This even works on the level of simple recognition. Think of the last time you bought a new car or even just a new pair of shoes. Suddenly, you see that color, brand, or style *everywhere*. It's not that those companies suddenly started producing or selling more of those cars or shoes. It's just that your RAS—now primed to see them—lets that information through. And the same will be true of Reset Moments because they are all around you all the time, and now you won't be able to help but see them.

Before digging more deeply into the benefits of this Mindset, let's revisit the components one more time.

Reset Moments are purposeful pauses to reflect and align actions with values, goals, and intentions. They are opportunities to rethink, reconnect, reinvigorate, and reprioritize.

Your *Reset Practice* is a simple three-step process to mine each Reset Moment for its treasure. 1. Step Back. 2. Get Perspective. 3. Realign.

The effective outcome of a sustained practice is your *Reset Mindset*. This foundational state of mind will keep you focused when solving problems, grounded when dealing with difficult situations, and open to innovation when pursuing significant goals.

Reset Moments are purposeful pauses to reflect and align actions with values, goals, and intentions.

The Value of the Reset Mindset

The practice of taking and making Reset Moments is invaluable to our mental and emotional well-being. It allows you to step back from the pressure and complexities of your business, helps you more effectively manage your people and metrics, and maintains your focus on the bigger picture.

More specifically, it will intrinsically provide the following value:

1. Thinking differently about change
2. Making the most of your time
3. Getting unstuck
4. Reaching objectives faster
5. Focusing on the right things

1. Thinking Differently about Change

Change is constant. It is futile to resist it. But you can learn to navigate it. Instead of dreading the inevitable, you can identify opportunity and growth.

Digging in your heels when change comes calling will lead you to ask yourself: Will I be able to keep up? Will I be left behind? Will I lose control?

But what if you reframed "change" simply as Reset Moments? What if you took a step back, gained perspective, and realigned to the new reality instead of sticking your head in the sand? Suddenly, change becomes an opportunity for rebirth, for growth, and for transformation. Change unlocks like a treasure chest, and inside you find innovation, valuable lessons, new methodologies, or actionable market insights.

Even more importantly, once you embrace change as a natural and essential part of life (and work), those feelings of overwhelm and lack of control that often accompany change . . . vanish! You become comfortable with uncertainty and the unforeseen. In a real way, you even start to look forward to change, even initiate change, and that's when your biggest gains come about.

Looking at change with a Reset Mindset will make you a more positive and proactive leader. This new view will also be the example you set for your team to do the same.

2. Making the Most of Your Time

No amount of time can be saved or used in advance. The past no longer exists. The future hasn't happened yet. There is only ever the present.

Yet, it's a constant struggle—we waste our present either fuming about the past or worrying about the future. Or, worst of all, we disengage and let autopilot lull us into complacency and spend our precious present with no intentionality.

In his book *Valvano: They Gave Me a Lifetime Contract, and Then They Declared Me Dead*, Jim Valvano said, "There are 86,400 seconds in a day. It's up to you to decide what to do with them." And once you spend those seconds, they are gone forever. If you think of those seconds as currency, how might you differently appreciate their value? How might you decide to invest them?

People like Bill Gates, Warren Buffet, Indra Nooyi, and Arianna Huffington say one of their secrets to success is to structure time for thinking, reflection, and introspection.

It may seem counterintuitive at first, but taking and making Reset Moments an investment in time. Carving out those moments of reflection will keep you more focused, resulting in greater speed and efficiency in the long run.

One of the best ways to create time is by investing time. Think of any activity or project as a s'more: the two graham crackers surrounding that gooey chocolate and marshmallow activity are the preparation and the debrief. Due to the state of distraction and urgency we live in, far too often, it's the debrief that we forgo. There aren't many things messier than an open-faced s'more!

Just like planning and preparation are valuable investments, the debrief is also essential. It is in this defined space where we can dissect what worked, what didn't, and what could be improved (even when things went well). A debrief sharpens our focus. It is the richest time, filled with lessons and learning to apply to the next challenge or step.

This simple act of reflection—this Reset Moment—may feel at first like a luxury, but in fact it is a powerful multiplier of efficiency and effectiveness. Debriefs save far more time than they cost. They are investments that pay off with bigger and bigger dividends the more you do them.

A debrief sharpens our focus.

We all have 86,400 seconds in a day. How are you spending them? When you budget them strategically—such as insisting on the debrief—you turn time into a tool instead of just a ticking clock.

3. Getting Unstuck

Have you ever felt stuck in a rut, or has your team's performance stagnated? Of course this has happened to you at some point. We all go through times when we feel like Sisyphus from Greek mythology, who was condemned by the gods for eternity to repeatedly push a boulder up a hill only to have it roll down again, never making progress. The monotony of checking boxes, attending useless meetings, and dealing with difficult people has people feeling disconnected and apathetic.

Stalling and stagnation are real problems for leaders,

workers, and companies. But an even bigger problem is when we don't even realize we're stuck. At those times, it's like we're sleepwalking through both work and life. Even if things are getting done, nothing of real meaning is getting accomplished, and life experiences become a chore instead of a joy.

My mentor, Peter, was a master at unsticking people (including me). I would come into his office frustrated, stressed, and blocked only to leave feeling refreshed, focused, and motivated. I was so eager to know his secret! So one day, I asked him, "How do you know just which buttons to push to motivate me?" He confidently answered, "I don't. The only person who can motivate you is *you*." That wasn't a new idea for me, but it sunk in when he said, "My job as a leader is to remove the obstacles that keep you from your motivation."

When I heard those words, a light bulb went on, and I understood a wider truth about focus. Peter helped me realize that while focusing on what matters most comes first, we must also identify *what prevents us from doing so*. There's a time to gaze at the forest, and there's a time to pinpoint a tree.

Around this time in my life, I read Eli Goldratt's novel *The Goal*. In this book, Goldratt outlines his "Theory of

Constraints," a methodology for identifying the limiting factors, or bottlenecks, which stand in the way of achieving a goal. I was struck by both the simple power of this theory and its similarity to Peter's philosophy of leadership.

Identifying and eliminating bottlenecks has been a part of my leadership and coaching process ever since. Cutting through the clutter gets you to the heart of where you need to focus. Ask yourself or your team these four questions and answer them honestly, and you'll be well on your way to eliminating the bottlenecks that slow you down:

1. What is your biggest distractor?
2. What takes the most time?
3. What wastes the most time?
4. What creates the most stress?

And guess what? Building a Reset Mindset orients you to look for the obstacles and other forces holding you and your team back. Remember, it's not about having all the answers all the time. It's about identifying the right questions for the situation. Back to Peter's earlier point: making the right decisions.

4. Reaching Objectives Faster

Getting unstuck means you'll be able to reach your objectives faster. Rather than forcing your way through a swamp, just go around. It may technically be a longer path, but it won't take nearly as much time.

Paul O'Neill became the CEO of Alcoa in 1987. His first speech to Alcoa's investors is now legendary. At the time, it seemed disastrous. "I want to talk to you about worker safety," he said to the crowd of Wall Street investors. Whoosh! The anticipatory energy drained out of the room. Into the uneasy silence, O'Neill continued. "Every year, numerous Alcoa workers are injured so badly that they miss a day of work. Our safety record is better than the general American workforce, especially considering that our employees work with metals that are 1,500 degrees and machines that can rip a man's arm off. But it's not good enough. I intend to make Alcoa the safest company in America. I intend to go for zero injuries."

The audience sat dumbfounded. Trying to get the meeting back to something resembling a Wall Street speech, a few veteran investors and business journalists asked questions about capital ratios and inventory levels. But O'Neill wasn't interested. Instead, he answered, "I'm not certain you heard me. If you want to understand how Alcoa is doing, you need to look at our workplace safety figures."

Everyone walked away scratching their heads. Investors scrambled to place sell orders of Alcoa stock. Journalists speculated that O'Neill had lost his mind.

Alcoa's employees, however, received the shock-wave message much more positively. Their safety was being prioritized over shareholder returns? Imagine the impact on worker morale and focus!

O'Neill's decision to pursue zero accidents was a major Reset Moment for the entire company. It was something that everyone at all levels of the organization could realign around. They had to slow down, pay more attention to the manufacturing process, and create the space for ongoing personal and collective reflection. Every time a safety issue was pinpointed . . . Reset Moment. Every time an assumption was challenged, every time the "way we've always done it" was scrutinized . . . Reset Moment.

To do the right things, you and your team first need to know you are focused on the right things.

Sure enough, the entire company built an entirely new mindset. More quickly than anyone could have anticipated, production, processes, and productivity improved. Focusing on worker safety led to innovation, more effective values, and a stronger culture.

Oh, and all those investors who sold? They quickly came to regret their decision. Alcoa's profits skyrocketed.

One purpose. One goal. One focus.

5. Focusing on the Right Things

A leader's first job is to ensure that the team is solving the right problem, just like Paul O'Neill saw that worker safety was the leverage point. This may seem obvious, but companies often are not aligned around the problem they claim to be solving.

I learned from another mentor of mine, Steve Linder, that the *presenting* problem is rarely the *real* problem. There is no greater productivity drain than chasing the wrong solutions because you failed to define the problem accurately on the front end. Peter Drucker says, "There is nothing so useless as doing efficiently that which should not be done at all."

To do the right things, you and your team first need to know you are focused on the right things.

One effective exercise is to ask each person on the team

to identify what they think the real problem is and why it exists. Share context. Compare answers. Dig deep. Challenge the presenting problem. Then, and only then, can you align around the right issues and set effective priorities.

Taking a Reset Moment to consider context ensures your focus has direction and purpose. Context creates *targeted* focus. Context connects you to the relevancy of bigger picture so your focus can help your broader goals and strategies come into alignment

Without context, focus is directionless.

with your actions. It's the difference between trying to do everything and intentionally doing the right things.

Without context, focus is directionless.

Many business leaders in their coaching sessions confessed to me they aren't as strategically focused as they would like to be. To put this in perspective, a study by the Strategic Thinking Institute confirmed that 96 percent of leaders questioned said they lacked strategic thinking time. As a result, leaders aren't able to maintain their focus on the right things, much less impart that focus to their team. So another exercise I suggest to my clients (and this one also ties back to making the most of your time) is to implement a "Time Audit."

A Time Audit is a kind of Reset Moment, one where you identify the gap between where you are spending your time operationally and where you need to be more strategic. (There are a number of different methods for a Time Audit. Mine is available at pennyskeynote.com/resources.) After the audit, you will gain new clarity about what you are doing and why you are doing it, and that clarity will enable you to rethink how you do it. You will also clearly identify the tasks that you can delegate.

One of my CEO clients, James, did a Time Audit and immediately realized that his presence at several meetings was not necessary. His presence, in fact, was disempowering his direct reports, because he was not allowing his leaders to be the drivers! He ended up reducing the number of meetings he attended *by half*. And the added benefit was that his leadership team felt more trusted and empowered. Productivity and engagement increased across the board. It might be worth asking what meetings you can and should stop attending.

Another one of my clients, Laura, did a Time Audit and likewise realized she was wasting large amounts of time in redundant one-on-one meetings. She created a new team meeting. Not only was time saved for her and her team, but the clarity of their communication improved dramatically.

Consistently—I might even say relentlessly—taking

and making Reset Moments such as aligning around the problem you are solving, defining the obstacles, preparing and debriefing properly, and taking Time Audits enables you to not only identify the right things but then also break them down into smaller, manageable steps. The ultimate goal always remains in sight, but by using this tool, you and your team can remain more flexible and adaptable, even as circumstances change.

The Reset Mindset will become your navigational tool, keeping you aimed at value-based outcomes.

Reset Exercise

1. What are some costs of not operating from a Reset Mindset, and conversely, what are concrete benefits you could experience in your life and leadership when you adopt one?

COST	BENEFITS

2. Describe a situation where things didn't turn out as you wanted (or presented as difficult or even impossible). What meaning did you give the situation, what did you feel, and how did you *react*? How could you have *responded* differently if you had taken a Reset Moment?

SITUATION	MEANING/ FEELINGS/ REACTIONS	OTHER POSSIBLE RESPONSES

3. Describe a challenging task or situation from your past that turned out in your favor. Write down the situation, the obstacles, and how you effectively handled it. What did you learn from that situation?

SITUATION	OBSTACLE	SOLUTION/ WORKAROUNDS/ LESSONS

CHAPTER 2

THE RESET MOMENT

I was in the Great Barrier Reef in Cairns, Australia, about to go on my first-ever nighttime scuba dive. A storm was brewing on the horizon. The sky was dark and looming, and the choppy sea rocked the boat side to side. The pounding wind and tumbling waves made me uneasy, even though I was scuba certified.

When I overheard one dive instructor ask another whether it was safe to dive, my stomach tied in knots. The approaching storm drowned out their words, but they must have agreed it was safe enough, because they called me forward. Barely able to balance, I made my way to the front of the boat and dove into the rough, angry water. I drifted and bobbed while waiting for the nine others to join me.

Suddenly, I realized the waves were dragging me far away from the boat and crew. I flailed my arms and legs, fighting helplessly against the current's drag. Panic overwhelmed me. *I didn't train for this! I'm in danger! People die at sea! I could die . . . I could really die.*

At that moment, I was trapped inside two raging seas. One was the actual salt water thrashing me around, and the other was the flood of terrified and self-defeating thoughts repeating themselves over and over in my head.

A wave took me under. As I sputtered to the surface, fear paralyzed me, and I knew that if I didn't regain control of my feelings and faculties quickly, I'd be in real trouble. The choice was clear: sink or swim.

I chose to swim.

Recalling my scuba training, I relaxed my body, which made me more buoyant and allowed me to take a few deep breaths. Those breaths slowed my heart rate. A slower heart rate lessened my panic. Even though I was buffeted by wind and rain, I managed to regain the ability to think clearly. I remembered that no matter how turbulent the surface, just a few feet down, the water would still be calm. That's the only reason the instructors would have continued the dive in these conditions, right?

With that change in thought, I pointed myself in the right direction and swam back to the group more easily. The situation hadn't changed, but my focus had. Letting go of fear allowed me to take back control.

That's the power of a Reset Moment. It gives you permission to create space, find clarity, and simplify. To shift your perspective when and where needed. Note that I'm not promising you *ease*. Reset Moments don't do the work for you. But they can show you what work is worth doing.

Again, Reset Moments don't have to be life-threatening, business-altering, or epic. In fact, the real work is in taking and making daily small ones. What mood we choose to start the day with. How we choose to respond to a coworker having a bad day. How we handle personal and professional disappointment or disagreement. How we approach a difficult conversation or difficult people. How we react when we're late for a meeting, or even when your child forgot to put out the trash *again*.

How we show up in the smaller moments will become the default for how we show up in the larger moments, when we need composure the most. Thankfully, given the stakes, that stormy night scuba diving wasn't my first time taking a Reset Moment. Because this had become my natural thinking pattern, I instinctively reached for my trusty tool when I most needed it.

Defining the Reset Moment

Let's get super clear. At its most fundamental, the Reset Moment is a purposeful pause for reflection, resulting in a conscious choice point. A moment to reconnect us to our objective and the people, projects, and priorities that matter most.

Note those words, "purposeful" and "conscious." There are potential Reset Moments around you all the time, but they snap into kinetic reality only once you *label* them. You've got to name them to access them fully. Purposefully and consciously carving out a pocket of time in the moment and labeling it a Reset Moment will give you the space to accept, understand, evaluate, and learn in real time.

A Reset Moment is also the literal time you take to activate your Reset Practice.

The amount of time can vary. Some Moments are mere seconds. Some may take a few minutes or even hours. And there are some pivots so consequential they take days, weeks, or even years to fully implement. These larger ones will have numerous smaller ones burrowed inside. Think of how long it takes an ocean liner to adjust course. The captain commands, "Turn left!" (or "Turn to port!"). There are thousands of tiny operations that then have to happen for that huge vessel to get her nose pointed in a new direction. Similarly, in your life or work, while some Reset

Moments will be as simple as a deep breath, an outside opinion, or a five-minute meditation, others will play out over much longer time frames.

There's no set number of Reset Moments you are "supposed" to take in any given day, either. They are meant to be flexible, to be useful to YOU, whatever your circumstance. So any time you feel lost in the chaos of your thoughts or swayed by distractions, or someone overreacts to something you said . . . take a Moment. Whenever you realize you are disengaged or unfocused . . . take another. When you are looking for inspiration and fresh ideas . . . that's a perfect time. Whenever your emotions threaten to overwhelm you . . . slow down, and take yet another. How do you want to show up? Within that purposeful pause, you'll be able to reassert control, direct your focus, and realign toward what truly matters.

In a world filled with endless stimuli, the Reset Moment is the ultimate strategy for filtering out the noise and zooming in on the essential.

The Power to Choose

There's a quote that's often attributed to Holocaust survivor Victor Frankl and megabestselling author Stephen R. Covey (the true origin seems to be a mystery) which is appropriate here: "Between stimulus and response, there is a space.

The power to choose our response is in that space. In our response lies our growth and our freedom."

That space that our mystery author writes of is where the Reset Moment lives.

Note that the quote uses the word "response," not "reaction." Reactions are instinctive and impulsive. They happen *prior* to thought. But a response *requires* intentional thought. While a reaction happens *to* us, we *choose* how we respond. Taking and making Reset Moments creates the space you need to choose your response.

Why is choosing our response essential to our "growth and freedom," our success and well-being? Why isn't simply reacting enough?

Reacting is an automatic, emotional response to a situation, usually performed without conscious thought or control. Past experiences, biases, and irrational emotions drive reactions. Because reactions are not based on a thoughtful or rational assessment of the situation, they often lead to negative outcomes and almost always cause dangerous escalation. In other words, while emotions are fleeting, consequences linger.

Responding, however, is an intentional and controlled way of handling a situation. Taking even just a few seconds to think about a situation and consider different options before taking action makes it more likely you'll achieve positive results and de-escalation.

Do you want your life and work to happen to you? Or do you want to be in charge of your choices and actions? Being in charge of your life and owning your focus are possible only in that space that the quote at the beginning of this section describes. You can't control or stop stimuli, but you can choose to respond rather than react. Another quote—this one actually from Frankl in his classic *Man's Search for Meaning*—sums this up better than I can: "When we can no longer change the situation, we are challenged to change ourselves."

Remember, taking these Moments when the stakes are low is just as important, if not more so, than taking them when the stakes are high. Low-stakes Reset Moments compound and prepare us for the bigger moments through practice and repetition. (More on compounding later!) Preparing for these bigger moments in advance helps us overcome them.

Proactive and Reactive Reset Moments

You've probably noticed by now that I've often used the phrase "take and make" Reset Moments. There is an intentionality behind these actions as both proactive and reactive.

The hardest part about taking Reset Moments is recognizing when to take them. What situations call for them? It's like the expression, "You can't see the forest for the trees."

You are so involved in the details that you may have lost perspective on the big picture of the situation. Much like building any new skill, it begins with awareness. You start to hone your noticing skills. At first, you might recognize it after the fact. The more you encounter and acknowledge these moments, the better you become at recognizing them when they appear. Over time, spotting Reset Moments becomes second nature.

You will see more opportunities to *make* more Reset Moments as part of your regular processes, meetings, and conversations. There's an advantage to being proactive in seeking them out *before* there is a desperate need for them. You can catch issues before they evolve into full-blown problems. You can identify trends and pivot to avoid a decline.

Proactive and visionary leaders don't wait for market changes, employee upheaval, or competitive pressure. They seek feedback early and often. They challenge assumptions. They listen for what's working and not working and remove obstacles that stand in their team's way. They help their people focus on what matters most and challenge their creativity to continually reinvent.

In this case, the motivating factor isn't fear or correcting what went wrong. Rather, the motivation is to create value, improve performance, gain a competitive advantage, generate innovations, enhance personal growth, and prevent adverse outcomes.

And here's the best news of all. You already know how to make Reset Moments!

They can be proactive (make) and reactive (take). The easiest way to understand the difference is this:

- Proactively making a Reset Moment is intentionally planning a check-in—scheduled meetings, policies and procedures, and any planned or recurring activity that creates the space to step back, gain perspective, and realign.
- Reactively taking a Reset Moment is signaling for a time-out, like in sports.

In sports, time-outs are typically used when things aren't going your way. You need to slow the other team's momentum, stop the clock, or take a moment to consider an alternate play or strategy. And just like a check-in, the time-out creates the space you need to take a step back, gain perspective, and realign to your goals, values, and objectives.

You probably already make Reset Moments in your personal life too. They may be formalized, like meditation or devotions. They may be more casual; simply the act of drinking your coffee or reading the newspaper in the morning. They could be taking your dogs for a walk or maintaining family dinner all together at the table. These are all highly recognizable and accessible Reset Moments.

Most professions already have various check-ins and time-outs built into their processes, too. You just have to learn to recognize them for what they are. Here are some examples:

In Law . . . Lawyers can request a *continuance*, which is a delay in proceedings so they can gather more evidence and better prepare their case. There's also a specific phase in litigation called discovery, where both parties have the opportunity to obtain evidence from each other. It's an intentional and essential space before trial for everyone involved to gather relevant information.

In Medicine . . . Before undergoing major procedures, patients often seek a *second opinion*. Getting a fresh set of eyes on their diagnosis can result in reassessment of treatment. Also, before medical research is published, it must undergo rigorous *peer review* by other experts in the field. This Reset Moment ensures the quality and accuracy of findings.

In Business . . . Before launching a product or service, companies conduct *market research* to gather data on potential success and make any necessary adjustments. Companies launching new initiatives or products will also often start with a *pilot program* in a controlled environment or specific region before investing in a full-scale rollout.

In Engineering and Construction . . . Engineers will engage in *feasibility studies* before embarking on major projects, to make sure the plans are viable. During construction, it's also vital to do regular *safety audits* to ensure all systems and processes are working safely and effectively.

In Finance . . . *Audits* are vital in finance as well, so that a company knows its financial statements are accurate and compliant. Before mergers, acquisitions, or other major investments, it's also vital for a company to do their *due diligence* and conduct a thorough appraisal to establish assets, liabilities, and commercial potential.

In Research and Academia . . . Just like in medicine, before publishing in a journal, a researcher's findings and methodology must undergo rigorous *peer review* by other experts in the field. And what is a *sabbatical* if not an extended Reset Moment? A chance for a professor to take a semester or year away from teaching duties to focus on research or improving their skills?

In Real Estate . . . Before a property is sold, it must undergo an *inspection* to determine its condition and identify potential issues. And before a price can be agreed upon, there has to be an appraisal, a professional *assessment* of a property's value.

In Technology and Software Development . . . *Beta tests* are vital to work out the kinks and eliminate bugs in new software before it's released to the general public. And much like peer review, other developers will do a *code review* before new code is integrated into the main code base, ensuring quality and functionality.

In Journalism and Publishing . . . Before a story is published, editors must *fact-check* the content to verify the accuracy of the information being presented. Similarly, even for fiction, editors must go through a manuscript to *proofread* and eliminate typos and mistakes.

All of these practices introduce deliberate pauses, debriefs, feedback points, safety checks, or controls into a workflow. They are each profession's version of a check-in or time-out, built into systems and processes to ensure perspective is gained and any necessary realignment is made.

Keep in mind that these are not stops. A check-in is an

intentional pause. Imagine you're driving a race car in the Indianapolis 500. At some point, you have to zip into the pit and refuel, change tires, and let your crew do the maintenance your high-performance car requires. You haven't stopped racing, but you've taken that intentional pause necessary to compete for the checkered flag.

Most of you already have these time-outs built into your business, so your job is simply to recognize them for what they are: institutionalized Reset Moments. When you label them and recognize them as such, you'll no longer just go through the motions. Instead, you'll maximize impact with this clear, underlying intention. The more you check in and take your time-outs, the more you will be building your Reset Mindset.

Institutionalizing the Reset Moment

The business world is fast-paced, no doubt. Our instinct is to move swiftly, pounce on opportunities, and stay ahead of our competition. Be aware there is a point where speed may actually slow you down. The value of integrating deliberate review points is immense. Making and taking Reset Moments is not a sign of hesitation, but rather demonstrates prudence, foresight, and a commitment to quality.

The benefits of institutionalizing Reset Moments in your business are numerous. You will mitigate risk. You will enhance quality. You will sharpen your decision-making. You will improve employee well-being, boost engagement, and reduce burnout. You will evolve more quickly as a leader because you'll be integrating the resulting feedback on a consistent basis.

So how can you integrate more Reset Moments into your processes? You, as a leader, need to institutionalize and normalize the concept. Here are a few actions you can take to advance this concept:

1. **Normalize the Pause.** Lead by example to show that Reset Moments are not interruptions but rather are crucial components of workflow. "Let's step back," or "Let's reset," should become a common shared phrase in your office. In each of your processes, identify the Reset Moments that already exist and review their relevance and evaluate other opportunities.

2. **Organize Feedback and Debriefs.** Solicit feedback at regular intervals and provide effective platforms for it to be analyzed, discussed, and implemented. Ensure structured debriefs take place after events, situations, and important outcomes. Have a defined process to make sure they are integrated into future actions. Lessons are found in reflection.

3. **Invest in Training.** Train on *when* and *how* to apply these concepts in your interactions, problem-solving and business processes,

   Lessons are found in reflection.

   encouraging a culture of continuous learning and adaptation. The training should also cover practical exercises and case studies to test and demonstrate the application and value.

4. **Measure and Trust Your Metrics.** Data is your ally. Reset Moments should be regular, but don't let them succumb to becoming "routine." Use data to inform when and where your time-outs should occur. Change them up when the data tells you to.

5. **Communicate the Why.** Make sure everyone understands not just the mechanics of Reset Moments but also their purpose and value. Highlight the many benefits. When your team sees the impact, they'll become more invested.

Remember, incorporating strategic check-ins and time-outs doesn't mean you are slowing down. It means you're moving forward with greater precision, sharper clarity, and heightened effectiveness. Just like in sports, a well-timed time-out can change the game.

Reset Exercise

Asking and answering these questions will help you build more awareness around different types of Reset Moments in both personal and professional areas.

1. Think back to your past week. What are some situations where you would have benefited from a Reset Moment personally or professionally?

Situation	Benefit	C/T*	C/P**

*C=Check-in, T=Time-out   **P-Personal C=Company

2. Reflect on where check-ins and time-outs already exist personally and professionally.

Situation	Benefit	C/T*	C/P**

*C=Check-in, T=Time-out   **P-Personal C=Company

3. How might you strategically implement more check-ins and time-outs? Think about this in the following areas: distractions, overwhelm, exhaustion, conflict, regret, creativity, gratitude and recognition, and joy and celebration.

_____

_____

_____

_____

_____

_____

_____

_____

_____

_____

_____

_____

_____

_____

_____

_____

_____

_____

_____

_____

CHAPTER 3

THE RESET PRACTICE

In February 2008, I was standing on the balcony of my family's Swiss chalet in Lenzerheide, admiring the breathtaking view. Lenzerheide is only about an hour and a half north of Zurich, where my husband and I lived. So we came to the mountains most weekends to ski in the winter and hike in the summer.

After a long day of skiing, I was taking in the sunset. I glanced over and smiled at the melting snowman in the balcony corner. My kids had built the frigid fellow earlier that weekend. And I suddenly had one of those moments where everything seems good. Successful in my career. Traveling the world. Healthy and happy children. A fifteen-year marriage. And my mentor, Peter, had taken me under his wing and was preparing me to take over as CEO.

Pinch me, right?

All the way down to our nanny. The children adored her. My hours were still such that having the extra help was incredibly fortunate. I went inside and helped her set the table for dinner.

And then . . . well. Someone pinched me.

As my husband poured the wine, I noticed that he poured our nanny's glass before mine. That tiny moment sent my brain into overdrive. I didn't sleep that night. The next day, my husband told me he didn't love me anymore.

Everything came crashing down. How did this happen? How did I miss this? My kids were one and three. What would divorce mean for them? Was this going to ruin their lives? What now?

I somehow managed to work despite the storm of emotion whirling around me and the great uncertainty of my family life. A few weeks later, Peter called the executive team into his office and gave us brutal news. GfK headquarters was selling our Swiss division to pick up an entity in Asia. We had just turned this division around, but it didn't matter. We were powerless, and because the sale didn't include senior management, we were about to be out of our jobs. Not only did we have no say in this change, but we were also tasked with implementing it. We felt like the carpet had been ripped out from under us.

To make matters worse, as my husband and I were

working through all the messy logistics of divorce, our financial advisor told us he had us invested with Bernie Madoff. Yes, *that* Bernie Madoff, the big Ponzi scheme guy. Most of our life savings . . . up in smoke.

In what felt like the blink of an eye, after that perfect moment on the balcony in Lenzerheide, everything I had worked so hard for—my family, my career, and my finances—was imploding, and I felt utterly powerless to prevent it.

When we feel personally and professionally defeated, how can we show up at our best for ourselves and others?

Though it was the most tempting course of action, what good would be accomplished if I were to wallow in self-pity? What effects would that have on my kids? No matter how terrible things were, when I needed it, my Reset Mindset enabled me to emotionally refocus, put things in perspective, and pay attention to what mattered. Daily, I would reaffirm my ideals and concentrate on the present-day variables that *were* in my control.

Daily, I would pull out that powerful question: What else does this mean? It would have been easy to say, "My husband is a liar and a cheat." And that would have been true. But for years, my husband had also been my mentor and friend. Just because *this* is true doesn't mean *that* isn't. And if both are true, then I can choose which I want to focus on. Because that choice will directly impact my attitude and how I show up. By asking, What else does this mean? I was able to show up with intention for my kids, for my coworkers, and, honestly, for *myself*.

But did you catch the catch? It has to be done DAILY. There is only one way to build your Reset Mindset, own your focus, and reclaim your sense of control . . . and that is through practice. A Reset Practice.

It's like Bruce Lee said: "I do not fear the man who has practiced ten thousand kicks one time. I fear the man who has practiced one kick ten thousand times."

The Secret of the Rubik's Cube

The Reset Practice is triggered by a Reset Moment. The distinction between a moment (or an event) and a practice is vital. Events are sporadic. A practice is ongoing. For example:

- A product launch is an event. Innovation is a practice.
- Goal setting is an event. Maintaining focus and prioritization is a practice.
- A team meeting is an event. Transparent communication is a practice.

- Hiring a new employee is an event. Fostering a positive company culture is a practice.
- Completing a project is an event. Collaborative teamwork is a practice.
- A Reset Moment is an event. Resetting is a practice.

These three steps are the practice:

1. Step Back
2. Get Perspective
3. Realign

Here is how we can visualize the power of this practice: When you STEP BACK, you are taking ownership and accountability. You are intentionally creating a distance between yourself and your biases, distractions, and old ways of looking at things. You are able to proactively observe your thoughts, actions, and experiences.

When you GET PERSPECTIVE, you are broadening and digging deeper to make connections, reassessing your options by seeking new inputs. You evaluate different perspectives and use the power of objectivity to break through resistance and limitations. Only by considering other perspectives can you challenge the status quo and open yourself up to maximizing potential.

STEP BACK

GET PERSPECTIVE

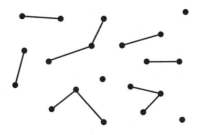

REALIGN

When you REALIGN, your broader viewpoint provides clarity on what drives the ladder of success. You block out the noise and reprioritize what matters most. Your actions and decisions realign with your values, goals, and new insights. It's a conscious decision to adjust your course in a way that resonates more deeply with who you are and what you aspire to achieve.

It's that simple. A three-step practice, repeated over and over, that moves you up the rungs of the ladder. Because here's the big secret: It's not about how complex a problem may be but how *simply* you approach it. Simplicity will ensure that this practice is quickly and readily available, no matter how stressful, uncertain, or emotional the situation.

The Rubik's Cube is a perfect example of how simplicity is the best approach to complexity. You might be surprised to know that no matter how jumbled a cube is, it can be solved by repeating the same few simple moves over and over. It doesn't matter where you start from. The same simple moves will solve the puzzle.

Even professional cube-solvers (yes, they exist!), for all their seemingly magical powers, are merely repeating a series of simple moves. Search "Rubik's Cube world record" on YouTube for some mind-blowing examples, but then go here* for the secret to the magic trick.

Whether it's a complex puzzle, your relationships, or the challenges in your life, the answer is the same—it isn't about how complex the problem is but how simply you approach it. The Reset Practice is simple. When you first start to implement these three steps, it can feel difficult, clumsy, or awkward—like anything new. But over time, with repetition, what seems difficult will begin to feel easy. The truth is: It doesn't actually get easier. You just get better at it.

Jocko Willink, a former Navy SEAL, in his book *Extreme Ownership*, unequivocally states that success is only possible through simplification. The more complicated the plan is, the more likely it will be to fail. If it's difficult to understand, or it takes too long to communicate the goals and strategies, or there are too many steps to effectively execute, success becomes less and less likely.

It may take more time and work on the front end to simplify things, but investing in simplicity yields higher efficiency and effectiveness no matter what field or endeavor you are involved in.

---

*"Learn How to Solve a Rubik's Cube 3x3 Steps," YouTube, accessed December 6, 2023, https://youtube.com/shorts/2sWEc0nYBFA?si=t3x6aVd6EcpqLmSj.

SEALs have a saying: "You don't rise to the occasion; you fall back on your training." In my TEDx talk, "The Energy of Thought,"* I played off that quote and said, "When under stress, we won't rise to the occasion, but we will sink to the level of our thinking."

The Reset Practice trains our thinking. No matter the complexity of the goal, the level of stress, or the difficulty of the situation, you can always fall back on these three simple steps to help you stay on track with your objectives, adapt to your environment, and reach your goals faster.

Step One: Step Back

In 1968, Bill Walsh became the offensive coordinator of the Cincinnati Bengals. At that time, the Bengals were in the basement. Their roster was made up of castoffs, players that the other NFL teams cut or didn't want. Also, their quarterback was notoriously inaccurate on throws longer than twenty yards. Walsh didn't argue with his reality, scream at the owners for more money, or blame the general manager for the limitations of the players. Instead, he took inventory of what he did have, and considered the possibilities. How else could he approach this?

---

*Penny Zenker, "The Energy of Thought." TEDxPSUBehrend, Tedx Talks, YouTube, June 9, 2017. https://youtu.be/lrQ5MJw3mss.

Realizing the offensive players available to him could not compete against NFL defenses using a typical NFL offense, Walsh developed an entirely new offensive scheme. He designed a playbook full of short and intermediate passes—twelve yards or shorter—to wide receivers running *precise* routes rather than routes that relied on speed or athleticism.

NFL defenses didn't know what hit them. By 1970, the Bengals were on top of the AFC Central. Walsh kept tinkering, and in 1979, he became head coach of the San Francisco 49ers, then the worst team in the NFL. Again, he took inventory and adapted his play-calling to his players, and he coached the 49ers to three Super Bowl victories. Even after he left the team, his now-legendary West Coast offense led to two more Super Bowls for the 49ers.

Beyond Cincinnati and San Francisco, Walsh's West Coast offense revolutionized the sport. Now teams intentionally run versions of his offense and seek out players who excel at the type of passing game he invented. But remember: he invented it because of the *limitations* of his players. He played to the strengths available, worked with what he had, created something far greater than the sum of its parts, and changed the entire game.

The first step in your Reset Practice—Stepping Back—is all about expanding your awareness and reconnecting with the big picture. Nothing can be accomplished if you don't know what you don't know or if you are unaware that you are directing time and resources in the wrong direction. Often, we'll get so focused on a task that we forget about the actual performance. Or we get so lost in our ego we lose sight of the real objective. Or we are so stuck in the problem we fail to focus on the solutions. Without the built-in pause and space of Stepping Back, there's no room for awareness to return.

Here are the four levels of awareness that Stepping Back can bring back into your work and life:

1. **Self-awareness:** This refers to your ability to recognize and understand your emotions, motivations, and biases, and how they may sabotage your intentions. Self-aware leaders can better manage their emotions and reactions, communicate more effectively, and make more-objective decisions.

2. **Situational awareness:** This refers to your ability to understand the context and dynamics of your current environment. Leaders with strong situational awareness can adapt to changing circumstances and make better-informed decisions to reach your goals faster.

3. **Cultural awareness:** This refers to your understanding of different cultures' values, beliefs, and customs. Leaders with strong cultural awareness can more effectively communicate and work with people from diverse backgrounds to achieve alignment around the overarching objectives.

4. **Stakeholder awareness:** This refers to your understanding of the needs and expectations of different stakeholders, such as customers, employees, and shareholders. Leaders with strong stakeholder awareness can more effectively manage and balance the interests of different groups without compromising the objective.

Stepping back is crucial. Without stepping back, you cannot gain clarity. You cannot disentangle yourself from emotions that cloud your judgment. And you cannot take inventory, like Bill Walsh did, with his simple assessment of team strengths (S), team weaknesses (W), game opportunities (O), and on-field threats (T). This process is known as a SWOT analysis and is very effective both when used individually and within a team.

But awareness is not enough. If we stop after step one, we get stuck in the knowledge gap, where we know what to do but aren't doing what we know.

Step Two: Get Perspective

The movie *Jaws* completely changed cinema by ushering in the age of the blockbuster. But the film's biggest draw—the shark—almost ruined the shoot.

The twenty-five-foot great white was actually three different animatronic models (affectionately and jokingly named "Bruce" after Steven Spielberg's lawyer), and they simply would not cooperate. They kept breaking down and malfunctioning, or they would just sink to the bottom during open-water shoots. It got so bad (and expensive!) that Spielberg started referring to Bruce as "the great white turd." Then still a young and relatively unknown film director, Spielberg realized he had to improvise and find other ways to build terror.

He ended up turning the camera itself into the shark's point of view. Remember the opening sequence, when the character Chrissie Watkins is swimming, gets attacked, and is ultimately pulled under to her death? It was scary! All of that suspense is built up *without ever even seeing the shark!*

Throughout the film, we get only glimpses of Bruce. We don't see him in all his twenty-five-foot glory until the very end, near the climax, when he devours Quint. The power of withholding is in full force. The suspense and terror are heightened by *not* seeing the shark for as long as possible.

And Spielberg figured out that storytelling hack only because Bruce wouldn't behave.

Challenges, constraints, and setbacks are a part of any business venture or life endeavor. But by stepping back, reassessing the situation, and looking at it from different angles, like Spielberg, we can find innovative solutions that might not only resolve the problem but also lead to better outcomes than initially envisioned.

Don't challenge the goal.
Challenge the assumption.

If Stepping Back is calling the time-out, then step two—Get Perspective—is the huddle on the sideline. It's the give-and-take between coaches and players, the review of what's been going on during the game and why things are (or aren't) going as intended. Everyone shares their points of view. Problems are identified. Solutions are offered. Perspective is gained.

My favorite guide for perspective-taking is a Neural Linguistic Programming (NLP) tool called Perceptual Positions. It is a tool used for understanding different points of view and improving communication and empathy. I also use it for creativity and new inputs.

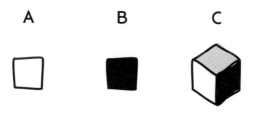

You start with an understanding that each position has a different viewpoint. You might think of it as each viewpoint being a side of the cube. Each side has a different color, which represents a clearly different perspective. In this graphic, your viewpoint is position "A," your counterpart's viewpoint is "B," and "C" is the proverbial "fly on the wall," observing all sides. If you have multiple parties, they could be B1 and B2, although each of them have their own point of view (represented by different sides of the cube). B could be an individual or a group you have a conflict, negotiation, or interview with, or it could be your competitor, or even your customer.

C isn't a person. C is a position. It's the viewpoint that takes into account both A and B (and B1, B2, B3, etc.). Position C is where you achieve a broad, objective view. You are able to see the whole cube and not just one side. C is where blind spots are uncovered, misunderstanding is corrected, conventional thinking is challenged, and creativity is explored. But you can only access the power of that objectivity when you step outside your own limited point of view. Only by seeing a situation from multiple perspectives by twisting, turning, and tilting the cube— from the C position—can you as a leader manage your teams, your competitors, and/or your market. You need to be on high alert against losing perspective, because the more power someone wields, the more distance there is between you and your people. And more distance leads to less understanding of how others think or feel, and what's really working—or not.

You can end up neglecting the concerns of your managers and employees because it's so easy to get caught up in the C-suite or your generational preferences. This may cost you the buy-in needed to align your team around the strategy or solution you are working toward. You must also understand that your power can be intimidating, and if you don't make a concerted effort to court their point of view, your employees may be hesitant to share their ideas or criticisms.

Soliciting their ideas and feedback might look like a workshop, a retreat, or even a survey that starts with you presenting the overarching strategy and getting their input on the implementation plan. When you communicate your goals clearly and why they are important, you are helping them best understand your view (position A). When you welcome and listen to input from them (position B), you open yourself to new ideas, which leads to more and better ideas. You ensure your employees feel valued and respected, which translates into ownership, loyalty, and enthusiasm for their work. And you create an atmosphere of investment and cooperation. Just make sure you communicate what you will do with that input and when, because a lack of follow-through may cause disconnection and disengagement.

Another reason to solicit their feedback? Well, this is a leadership secret that isn't really a secret, but it bears saying: *You don't know everything.* As a leader, you may feel the pressure to have all the answers all the time. But nothing could be further from the truth. True leadership means having the humility and courage to consider perspectives other than your own and to seek the best result for the greater good—even if it is not self-serving.

Being more informed and maintaining a broader view will also lead to stronger, faster, and fairer decision-making. By welcoming a variety of perspectives, you can reduce assumptions, biases, and stereotyping, both within yourself and within your business. By understanding what is driving people, you can more effectively de-escalate tense situations and resolve conflicts faster. Creativity, innovation, and cooperation all accelerate when leaders show a willingness to listen and engage.

Just like in negotiations, understanding where the other party is coming from and what is driving them can help you come to the best agreement. You don't have to *agree* with their point of view as long as you *understand* it. The cube analogy from NLP's Perceptual Positions framework is based on seeking to understand, not to be understood. FBI negotiator and bestselling author of *Never Split the Difference,* Chris Voss, has a very clear barometer for when you've made a true connection and gained mutual understanding. He recommends you not be satisfied with their merely replying, "You're right." *You're right* simply means they are done with the conversation, not that they agree with you. What you want to hear is "That's right." *That's right* means the other person feels heard, and you have made a real connection. Empathy for other people's view reduces stress and avoids unnecessary escalations.

An effective way to get to *That's right*—which is really just a version of position C—is to ask those simple yet powerful questions I mentioned earlier: *What else?* And *How else?* These simple questions continually nudge you out of A and your counterpart out of B, allowing you both to find C. There are many other questions and frameworks that can support your obtaining and maintaining a broader view; see the Afterword for more options.

Most importantly, this framework will help you regulate your emotions at work and at home. Sometimes emotions can be so overwhelming they hijack us, making us incapable of rational thought and provoking uninhibited, negative responses. There's a concept in Buddhism that embodies this condition: the *monkey mind*. When our monkey mind takes over, we get restless and act capriciously; we lack control over our thoughts and choices. From neuroscience we know that perspective-taking activates the executive functions of our brains, giving us quicker escapes from times of emotional hijacking. So by engaging in this step—Get Perspective—we can reassert control whenever our monkey mind tries to take over.

Finally, the benefits of mindfulness have begun to be

recognized across all layers of society, and perspective-taking is another way to practice mindfulness. The emphasis on reflection, being present, and accepting situations without judgment grounds us and diverts our energies away from negative stressors and counterproductive, reactive states of being.

Don't waste your time-outs. Don't go with the first play in the playbook. Challenge the status quo, seek new voices, look at things from different angles, and challenge assumptions.

Step Three: Realign

On May 6, 1954, a young medical student named Roger Bannister accomplished the unthinkable: he ran a mile in under four minutes. At that time, most people believed the human body was incapable of achieving such a feat. After all, professional runners and athletes couldn't do it, so what made an amateur think he could?

Bannister's approach was to focus not simply on his physical prowess but also on the mental aspects of running. He put his body through the necessary training, of course. But he also aligned his thinking, his behaviors, and his environment. He continually sought feedback from himself and his team. He stayed focused on what mattered most and achieved something no one else in history had ever done.

The more focused
you stay on what
matters most, the less
distracted and burned
out you will be.

The experts thought it would be possible only in perfect weather—68 degrees, no wind—and on a hard, dry track in front of a huge crowd urging the runner on. But Bannister, ignoring the experts and trusting his own constant realignment, broke the barrier on a cold day, on a wet track, in front of a small crowd.

The true moral of the story, though, is that while runners had been officially chasing the four-minute mile goal since 1886, once Bannister broke through in 1954, he and another runner did it again just *forty-six days later*. That's sixty-eight years to break it once and a month and a half to break it again. Bannister's achievement didn't realign just his own thinking but also every other runner's in the world. A year later, three runners broke the barrier *all in the same race*. Since then, another 1,750 athletes have officially run a mile in under four minutes.

If step one is calling the time-out (Step Back), and step two is huddling up (Get Perspective), then step three is sending the team back out into the game with new strategies (Realign). How's that old saying go? "Insanity is doing the same thing over and over again and expecting different results." No coach keeps their job for long if they keep running a play that the opposing defense stuffs every time. Activating the Reset Practice culminates in Realignment, in calling a new play.

Easier said than done, though. How do we align our team's attention with project goals when they are already overloaded and overwhelmed with day-to-day activities and distractions? This is where Reset Moments come in. Individually and collectively, as a leader, you must create the space to realign. Realignment is not a one-and-done event. It is about continuous reassessment. Remember, the three steps make the complex simple. You must call the time-outs, lead the huddle, and send the team back out after realigning them with the shared goal.

Here's the most powerful thing about Realignment: it inherently triggers a feedback loop. Each time

You must create the space to realign.

you walk through the steps, you are adapting and aligning around what matters most. Every realignment will bring you closer and closer to achieving your goals. The more focused you stay on what matters most for reaching your intended goal, the less distracted and burned out you will be.

Three Reset Practice Examples

As you begin to take and make more and more Reset Moments in your life and work, you will discover that your Reset Practice can manifest in a wide variety of ways.

I've mentioned a few already. Asking yourself, *What else could this mean?* is, unto itself, a Reset Practice. So is asking, *How do I want to show up?*, *What problem are we solving?*, or *How else might we accomplish this?* Asking questions such as these activates the practice.

So here are a few day-in-the-life examples of Reset Moments and Practices. You may recognize yourself or some moments and practices you already do, and that's great. That means your next step is to *label* it. You'll recall that nothing happens until you intentionally and consciously *name* something a Reset Moment. The awareness creates the space and activates the practice.

A Day in the Life: Adrian

As the first glimmer of sunlight pierced the blinds, Adrian's alarm clock blared. His hand reached out, fingers hovering between the "snooze" and "off" buttons. *Reset Moment #1: Wake up with the alarm.* Adrian chose "off" and swung his feet out of bed, starting the day with forward energy and respecting the decision he made the night before when he set the alarm. He enjoyed the extra space of his mornings, priming himself for the day ahead with some stretching and reflection. If he had chosen "snooze," not only would he have missed out on all the benefits of the practice, but he would have also found himself rushing and feeling anxious.

As he exited his building, Adrian caught the scent of coffee wafting from a street vendor's cart. Even though he'd usually grab a to-go cup on autopilot, he remembered his intent to reset this morning. *Reset Moment #2: Plan for the day.* So instead, he chose a sit-down breakfast at a nearby café to give himself a quiet moment to plan and mentally prepare for the day.

As Adrian drove to work, a sedan swerved into his lane, causing him to slam on his brakes. His heart raced, and he felt the urge to shout and gesture aggressively at the other driver, but he remembered the power of a pause. *Reset Moment #3: Assume positive intent.* So he took a deep breath . . . and chose empathy. "Maybe they're having a rough morning," he thought, and drove on with added caution.

At the office, a colleague told Adrian his 10:00 a.m. presentation had been rescheduled to 9:00 a.m. No heads-up, no time to prepare. Panic crept in. But before it took hold, *Reset Moment #4* emerged: *Focus on the outcome.* He found a quiet space, closed his eyes, visualized success, and reminded himself of his strengths and capability. He also realized how taking that extra time earlier in the morning was having a cumulative and ongoing effect. The meeting went smoother than expected, and his impromptu agility earned him praise.

Later in the day, as the clock raced against his project deadline, the pinging of emails and chat notifications broke his concentration. It was a tempting distraction. Why not take a small reprieve from the stress? However, *Reset Moment #5* beckoned: *Realign with the objective of this work segment.* Instead of diving down the rabbit hole of unread messages, he set a timer for forty-five minutes and reclaimed his focus.

As Adrian got home from work, his dog, Max, bounded up, excited and eager for attention. Adrian's hands were full of mail, and his phone was lighting up with work notifications. Pulled in different directions, he realized this was *Reset Moment #6: Time to recharge.* He turned off his phone, tossed the mail on the table, and took Max for a walk. At the park, they even played a little fetch. That break provided laughter and relief. He returned home recharged.

As Adrian reflected on his day, he realized that every challenge and unexpected twist offered him an opportunity: the chance to reset, to choose response over reaction. Life wasn't about avoiding these moments but embracing and mastering them.

A Day in the Life: Leah

Leah, a driven leader at a fast-growing tech firm, was accustomed to days packed with back-to-back meetings, decision-making, and people management. But after several weeks of feeling burned out and like she was always behind and never able to catch up, she made a pact with herself to recognize and capture Reset Moments—to ensure she was being both an effective leader at work and a present wife and mother at home.

One morning, as Leah was reviewing a report to prepare for the day's first call, her youngest, Mia, tugged at her blouse. "Mommy, can you help with my shoe?" Even though her mind was already focused elsewhere, she recognized *Reset Moment #1: Work doesn't start until she leaves the house.* So Leah set aside the report and helped Mia, creating a brief but cherished mother-daughter connection.

When she arrived at work, Leah found her team in a heated discussion about the direction of a certain project. Instead of diving in or letting emotions dictate the room, she invoked *Reset Moment #2: De-escalate emotional reaction.* She paused the meeting and initiated a five-minute silent brainstorming session. The change in dynamics allowed everyone to step back, recalibrate, and express their thoughts constructively. A few minutes later, they came up with an agreed-upon criterion to make further directional decisions, and everyone left feeling upbeat and productive.

During lunch, Leah learned a critical vendor had pulled out, jeopardizing an important launch. As her anxiety climbed, she remembered *Reset Moment #3: Focus on what you can control. Look for other options, and seek outside counsel.* She stepped outside for a brief walk, cleared her mind, and called a colleague, who helped her identify a creative solution that even improved the original plan.

In the late afternoon, Leah got a message that her eldest, Lucas, had been in a minor accident at school. The instinct to panic threatened to overwhelm her, but she activated *Reset Moment #4: Don't make assumptions*. She left a message for her husband, saying she would be home as soon as she could.

Heading home, stuck in traffic, her mind bounced back and forth between Lucas and the unopened emails piling up. This was her *Reset Moment #5: Intentional transition to home*. She reclaimed this window as an opportunity to listen to a podcast. The frustrating commute transformed into a time of relaxation and learning.

When she got home, the kids ran up. Lucas sported a small bandage on his arm but was otherwise fine and excitedly told the story of how he'd been climbing the monkey bars. Mia held up a drawing she had made, demanding Mommy's artistic verdict. Their energy and the chaos of home could have easily felt overwhelming, which triggered *Reset Moment #6: Smile and feel the gratitude*. She hugged Lucas, ensuring he was okay, and sat down with Mia to celebrate her artwork. She could follow up with the emails later. This was family time.

Later, as she lay in bed with her husband, Leah remarked

on the power of these Reset Moments not just to navigate work's demanding tides but also to ensure that the truly important things—family and personal well-being—were not sidelined.

A Day in the Life: Ethan

Ethan was an employee known for his versatility, working on multiple projects managed by different leaders across departments. His ability to juggle diverse tasks was commendable, but the challenge of competing priorities under tight deadlines was becoming overwhelming.

His day began with an influx of emails from both project teams, each marking their tasks as urgent. Ethan felt the pressure mounting. This was his *Reset Moment #1: Prioritize first.* Instead of diving headfirst into the tasks, he took a moment to breathe and prioritize. He made a list, categorizing tasks by urgency and impact, allocating specific times in the day for each project, and being mindful not to allow the urgent to crowd out the impactful. He clearly defined one impactful task for each project and scheduled it. This organization gave him a clear path forward amidst the chaos.

Midmorning, during a project meeting for Team A, a critical issue was raised that threatened to derail their deadline. Ethan recognized this as his *Reset Moment #2: Speak up.* Although he was the junior on the project, he spoke up and proposed a focused brainstorming session, inviting fresh perspectives from the team. This collaborative approach quickly led to an innovative solution, keeping the project on track without sacrificing quality.

As he switched to working on tasks for Team B, Ethan received an urgent call from Team A needing immediate assistance. Here was his *Reset Moment #3: Urgency Protocol: Negotiate timelines.* He assessed the situation and realized that responding to Team A's issue would severely impact his commitment to Team B. He communicated this openly to both teams and negotiated a slight adjustment in deadlines that was agreeable to all. This honest and transparent communication helped manage expectations and maintain trust.

In the afternoon, Ethan found himself struggling to concentrate, pulled in different directions by the demands of both projects. His *Reset Moment #4: Take a break.* He acknowledged the need for a brief break. He stepped away from his desk for a short walk, allowing his mind to rest. This short respite recharged him, boosting his productivity for the rest of the day.

As the day drew to a close, he had *Reset Moment #5: Evaluate performance reflections.* Ethan reflected on his accomplishments and challenges of the day. He felt a bit disconnected from his work lately. This led to a recognition of a pattern of overcommitment from eagerness to please and not wanting to rock the boat. In an effort to better manage his workload, he decided to have a discussion with both project leaders about setting realistic expectations and timelines. This proactive approach would help him avoid an inevitable burnout and create a more sustainable balance for future projects.

Ethan's story illustrates the power of Reset Moments in managing competing priorities. By taking steps to organize, collaborate, communicate transparently, take necessary breaks, and set realistic expectations, he navigated his multifaceted role with resilience and efficiency.

Note not just the *amount* of Reset Moments that Adrian, Leah, and Ethan took in those examples but also the *variety* of Reset Practices that those moments activated.

Some of them were proactive and intentional, like Adrian choosing a wake-up time or Leah keeping work and home time separate. You could think of these as self-imposed rules, but not rules that limit. These rules support our objectives and allow us to detach. They act as boundaries. They ease anxiety and remove the stress of having to make choices under stress, because you've already made the choice in advance. As a colleague once said to me, "Make a rule when you're cool; break it not when you're hot." These rules ensure we comply with what's most *important* to us in the long run, not what's *easiest* in the moment. It forces us to think about what values we want to prioritize and how we want to pursue our objectives. They eliminate decision fatigue, offset willpower, and keep you focused on the right things.

Other practices in the examples above were situational, or reactive. These are things beyond our control that we can still choose our response to—like Adrian's meeting being rescheduled, or Leah's son having an accident, or Team A calling Ethan for immediate assistance.

This is one of the most important aspects of Reset Practices. They are *flexible*. They can adapt to any particular situation. There are so many ways you can apply a rule, use a different filter, or get unstuck; you simply have to label them. As simple as this sounds, Reset Practices are simply brain hacks that get us out of our own way.

They can even be "body hacks" that reset your brain and emotional state through something physical, like Adrian playing fetch with his dog or Ethan stepping out for a quick walk. Exercise, a plunge in a pool or pond, lighting a scented candle, or even just some light stretching—engaging your physiological self can have a great impact on your psychological self.

So whether it's asking questions, making rules, using frameworks, investing in habits, doing something physical, or repeating mantras, affirmations, and inspirational quotes, you can infuse your day-to-day with opportunities to show up exactly how you want to.

Reset Exercise

Reflect on the various Reset Practices already woven into your life and work. When do you call your time-outs? What rules, frameworks, or affirmations do you already utilize? Write them down and describe them. Then assess what new Reset Practices you'd like to add to your life and work. Write them down and describe them.

EXISTING RESET PRACTICES	POTENTIAL NEW RESET PRACTICES

CHAPTER 4

RESETTING YOUR MIND

In 2020, I had a client, Todd, who wanted to grow his speaking and consulting business. He spent *weeks* posting on LinkedIn, trying to gain some traction. Things looked bright as the engagement, comments, and positive interactions all increased.

After gaining this initial momentum, he wanted to take his game to the next level. He invested significant funds into a formal video-recording setup and spent many hours a day scripting and editing. I couldn't help but wonder whether all that time and expense had been worth it compared to the return on investment. Was Todd focusing on what mattered most?

I asked Todd to think about the goal he wanted to achieve with these videos. Todd first became defensive (as most of us would!). He explained that high-quality videos were now all the rage and that in order to gain clients, he had to spend all this time and money. That wasn't my experience of the trend. I didn't have the stats at the time, but most people today prefer and engage with real-world videos shot on the spot—everything from people driving in their cars to walking down the street to cooking or doing other natural things in their day-to-day lives.

I suggested he try some unscripted, off-the-cuff videos, test both variations, and measure the likes, comments, and interactions he achieved with each. Reluctantly, he tried it out. Game changer! The off-the-cuff videos resulted in *double* the interaction compared to the slick, "commercial-y" ones. Afterward, I looked it up, and surveys have shown that 78 percent of users got more traffic to their sites after using creative, "real-world" video content; 83 percent generated more leads, and 44 percent increased sales.

It's vital to differentiate between task management and performance management. Todd was so focused on perfecting his videos that he lost sight of his true goal. The goal wasn't to make great, quality videos but to create value for his followers and convert them into clients.

It's vital to differentiate between task management and performance management.

In the following weeks, Todd told me this insight saved him ten hours a week and transformed how he approached the rest of his business and personal life. He said, "There isn't a day that goes by that I don't think of your words about being stuck in the task, and that I needed to stop managing the task and start managing performance. Now I'm constantly questioning my behaviors at work and home to see that I focus on the things of the highest value."

Let's reflect on Confucius's quote "He who chases two rabbits catches none." Well, Todd was making the ancient, common mistake of chasing two rabbits. Lots and lots of activity, effort, and energy spent. Nothing to show for it.

At first glance, one might interpret Confucius's wisdom as advocating for singular focus: chasing just one rabbit for maximum productivity. Yet through my personal pursuit of various rabbits over the years, I've uncovered a deeper truth: productivity isn't the point. When we get lost in the chase, we lose sight of the true objective, and the chase itself becomes a distraction from what truly matters. Impact happens when we *catch* the rabbits.

If you want to catch more rabbits in less time with less effort, then don't waste time perfecting the chase.

Focus on catching.

The snappy business-jargon way to think of this is "work smarter, not harder."

There's a fun exercise I do during my live keynote speech to illustrate this point. A volunteer will come up and play hide and seek. They will close their eyes while I hide the Rubik's Cube somewhere in the room. Then, I give them ninety seconds to find the object. The audience is observing in discomfort as the person struggles, searching here and there.

Don't waste time perfecting the chase.

When the volunteer inevitably fails to find the cube, I ask them what would have helped. They had a clear goal, so it wasn't more clarity. More time? No. Searching faster?

No. Greater effort? No. They are left feeling frustrated, depleted, and alone.

Then I'll update the rules. I'll tell the audience to call out "hotter" or "colder" as the volunteer searches again. You probably remember a version of this game from childhood. The energy of the room changes. It becomes like the audience screaming prices at contestants on *The Price Is Right*. I set the same time limit, but you know what happens? The volunteer, taking the "hotter-colder" feedback from the audience, finds the cube in just a few seconds. One small change—adding structured feedback—and the game goes from being almost impossible to impossibly simple. Just taking those split seconds to listen to the audience feedback and adapt accordingly.

You know what those split seconds are, when the volunteer tunes in to what the audience is saying?

You got it. Those are Reset Moments. During this game, you see it happen in real time. The volunteer, in real time, dynamically pauses with each few steps to listen, get perspective from the audience, and realign direction as needed. And without fail, the volunteer finds the hidden cube in record time.

The Reset Mindset is the ultimate version of "work smarter, not harder."

The Beliefs of a Reset Mindset

In chapter 1, I compared a mindset to a computer's operating system. Another way to think about your mindset is that each cluster of beliefs is a filter. You see the world and take in all the information through these filters. Obviously, those belief filters hold the power to influence not just *what* you think but *how* you think. The choice of filters can open up your mind, world, and business . . . or cripple them.

Here are some of the filters you'll experience once you build a Reset Mindset. These ways of thinking—these clusters of beliefs—are the true purpose behind doing this work.

1. Change Is Constant
2. Stay Open to Possibilities
3. There Is No Failure, Only Feedback
4. Assume Positive Intent
5. Risk Improves Luck
6. Permission to Let Go

Belief filters hold the power to influence not just *what* you think but *how* you think.

Change Is Constant

Change does not happen on our schedule. According to author Peter Drucker, "The greatest danger in times of turbulence is not the turbulence; it is to act with yesterday's logic." I would add that "times of turbulence" are the rule, not the exception. Change is not only always coming; it's always happening. And if we have any hope of recognizing—much less adapting to—it, we must first simply accept it.

On an even more proactive level, the Reset Mindset ensures that you'll not only be ready to *respond* to change but also be looking to *implement* change. If change is going to happen anyway, why not be on the front end? Why not be the *cause*?

Also, understand that it's not just the world of circumstances that changes. YOU change, whether you want to or not. It's inevitable. So why not embrace it? Take the opportunities to reinvent yourself, improve and learn, and transform constraints into catalysts.

Seeing the world through the filter of "Change Is Constant" is one of the surest ways to be an effective leader.

Stay Open to Possibilities

This filter ensures you'll remain willing to question assumptions, challenge the status quo, and consider opportunities that may not, at first blush, appear popular or comfortable.

In 1921, the slogan for Kirby's Pig Stand in Dallas, Texas, was "A delightful meal, served at your wheel." Because the restaurant had no dining room, carhops would deliver meals to customers in their cars. Kirby's was having moderate success with this model, but then the founder, Jesse Kirby, noticed a trend: people weren't just *putting up* with eating in their cars. They actually *preferred* it to going inside!

So Kirby took a chance, even though many in the industry scoffed. He opened the world's first drive-through window. Talk about a game changer! Today, drive-throughs are ubiquitous. McDonald's reports that their drive-throughs account for roughly 70 percent of business.

All because Jesse Kirby stayed open to possibilities and asked, *How else might we?*

There Is No Failure, Only Feedback

Author Robert Allen said, "There is no failure. Only feedback." There are any number of other ways to express this sentiment. Similarly:

Henry Ford: "Failure is only the opportunity to begin again, only this time more wisely."

Samuel Beckett: "Ever tried. Ever failed. No matter. Try again. Fail again. Fail better."

Japanese proverb: *Nana korobi, ya oki* ("Fall down seven times, stand up eight.")

But it's Robert Allen's reframing of failure as *feedback* that best fits the Reset Mindset. Once you see the world through this filter, you'll realize that setbacks are never endpoints. Rather, they are opportunities. Opportunities to grow and learn.

In business and life, we are terrified of being labeled "failures." But the Reset Mindset makes you incapable of being a failure, not because you won't experience failure (you absolutely will) but because you'll be able to unwrap the gift hidden inside every failure: feedback. Failure will transform from hang-your-head end points to blow-your-hair-back propulsion systems.

The true test of your Mindset will be if you can put your ego aside and accept the feedback for what it is: guidance.

Remember the hide-and-seek, "hotter-colder" example? The collective goal wasn't for my volunteer to fail over and over again but to receive feedback and act upon it. To be effectively guided to the goal. Having the team yell "Cold!" at you is not failure. It's feedback.

Assume Positive Intent

This filter has helped me transform numerous negative situations into positive ones, including employee conflicts, business setbacks, and even tricky situations with friends.

For example, I had an adversarial relationship with a colleague (let's call him Pierre) on the executive team at GfK. My initial experiences with Pierre led me to believe he was out for himself, with his eye on the position of CEO. Working with him was emotionally draining, combative, and unproductive.

It wasn't until I met with a coach that I realized I was part of the problem. I wasn't giving Pierre the benefit of the doubt when he had to cancel a meeting or send one of his team members in his place. I was assuming the worst and making it personal, and every time I did that, I built the wall between us a little higher.

My coach helped me take the time to reset and see Pierre's perspective. He wasn't out to get me. He had pressures and challenges of his own. From that point forward, having adjusted my mindset, I didn't take things personally or automatically have an adverse reaction. I was less stressed and more optimistic about our work together. The dark cloud of my frustration, anger, and resentment lifted, and working together became easier. Significantly, shortly after I changed *my* behavior, he changed *his*. That is the power of assuming positive intent.

In her book *Dare to Lead*, Dr. Brené Brown wrote, "Daring leaders, work from the assumption that people are doing the best they can; leaders struggling with ego, armor, and/ or a lack of skills do not make that assumption." From my own experience, I've learned that giving people the benefit of the doubt focuses you on the result, the gap or behavior, and not the person. Interpreting other people's actions, words, and intentions generously is not an easy skill to learn or practice, but it is essential in your business and life if you want to live a happier life. This filter reduces conflicts, strengthens relationships, and forges a greater sense of community. Trust me. Taking this approach is much more effective than avoiding confrontation or ignoring conflict, especially because whichever approach you decide to take—positive or negative—will almost always come back to you, amplified.

Ken Chenault, the former CEO of American Express, affirms this point: "When we assume positive intent, we create a space for better communication and understanding." So find the common ground, listen to others' perspectives, identify the source of any misunderstanding, and be open to compromise. Mutually beneficial solutions do exist, and you can find them with a Reset Mindset.

Risk Improves Luck

"Risk" and "luck" used to be taboo four-letter words among businesses and leaders. Risk meant dangerous, and luck meant unskilled.

But risk is not only normal—it's necessary. In the commencement speech at Johns Hopkins University in 2014, former YouTube CEO Susan Wojcicki said, "Life doesn't always present you with the perfect opportunity at the perfect time. Opportunities come when you least expect them or are not ready for them. Rarely are opportunities perfectly presented in a nice little box with a yellow bow on top. Opportunities, the good ones, are messy, confusing, and hard to recognize. They're risky. They challenge you."

Looking at your business (and life) through a Reset Mindset, you will be equipped to differentiate smart, calculated risks from what is merely "risky." And just because you'll still sometimes "lose"—like in poker, when you might play a hand perfectly, but that last card goes the wrong way—it doesn't mean taking that risk was bad or wrong.

Here's the other thing about risk or making any bet: you can't win if you don't play. You can't be the beneficiary of that "lucky" last card if you've already folded.

As the Stoic philosopher Seneca said, "Luck is simply what happens when preparation and courage meet opportunity." Especially if you have already reframed failure as feedback, then smart risk-taking has been stripped of its power to paralyze you. Remember Kirby's drive-through window? It's easy to look back now and see how obviously successful that choice would become. But at that moment, Kirby was taking a risk. A smart, calculated risk, to be sure, but his drive-through window could have failed. Was he just "lucky"? A jealous competitor might think so, but really, Kirby's "luck" was simply the result of taking the risk.

Permission to Let Go

In 2008, while I was struggling with the emotional turmoil from my divorce, a friend of mine suggested I write in a journal. Specifically, my friend encouraged me to write down every detail of how my husband had wronged me. Get it out; get it all out. I did take the advice to start writing in a journal, but that angry approach instinctively felt wrong. What we focus on expands. I knew writing that way would simply fill me with anger and resentment. That would not have helped me get past my ego and make good decisions for myself, my kids, and my colleagues. It wasn't about being right but about getting it right.

To get it right, we have to let go of being right. When you focus on a greater purpose than yourself, it makes it easier to let go.

Listening to an Oprah *Super Soul Sunday* series about simple abundance with Sarah Ban Breathnach turned me on to the

To get it right, we have to let go of being right.

power of gratitude. So, I decided to journal every day and write down three things I was grateful for. And that was a lifesaver. Some days, it was hard to come up with three, but the more you look for it, the more you find. I consistently maintained that journal for ten years.

But at some point, I noticed that even though I was writing things down, the emotional connection wasn't the same. It had become an activity that had to be done—like an obligation—rather than something that served me. I knew I needed to do something different in order to regain that element of tapping into the power of gratitude.

So I let the journal go.

I have come to learn that things work until they don't, and we need to continually check in to reaffirm whether they're still working as intended.

So I mixed it up. Instead of journaling, I varied my gratitude-inspiring activities. I started writing letters to people; we'd go around the dinner table saying what we were grateful for; I whispered in my sleeping children's ears the strengths I saw in them; and I made sure I gave three purposeful compliments a day to people in my life. And remember, another reliable way to look at gratitude is simply to accept what is and let go of what we think should be.

Even in my darkest moments, when I felt like I was losing everything—my family, finances, and career—I worked to take back control of my emotions, choices, and connection to what mattered most. But to do so, I had to let go of my expectations of future outcomes. To avoid frustration, I had to let go of my expectations of my children's father when he didn't show up for them. To show up in favor of my children, I had to let go of my anger. And let go of what people might think. Just let go.

This is perhaps the greatest benefit of building a Reset Mindset: the power to give yourself permission to let go. Letting go allows us to embrace open-mindedness, possibility, and humility. Letting go of the old creates space for the new. Letting go reframes negative experiences so you can leave mistakes behind instead of dragging them along. Letting go jettisons unrealistic expectations and releases things we cannot change. Letting go brings stability, relief, and emotional balance. Letting go sets you free and opens you up.

When you let go, you understand that all you have is the present. And that is enough.

Things work until they don't. We need to continually check in to make sure they're still working as intended.

Reset Exercise

Review the beliefs of the Reset Mindset and consider how they manifest in your life.

BELIEF	WHERE I'VE SEEN THIS BELIEF MANIFEST IN MY LIFE
Change Is Constant	
Stay Open to Possibilities	
No Failure, Only Feedback	
Assume Positive Intent	
Risk Improves Luck	
Permission to Let Go	

CHAPTER 5

ONE RESET MOMENT AT A TIME

Albert Einstein is said to have once hailed compound interest—interest earned on interest payments that have already been made and added to a principal sum—as "the greatest force in the universe." You'll recall from chapter 1 how I struggled when I joined GfK after experiencing burnout from years of running my own successful company. I thought the new job would make things better—make *me* better.

But as Jon Kabat-Zinn famously wrote, "Wherever you go, there you are." The problems weren't external. Stress. Anxiety. Lack of control. All of them had compounded inside me each year—one building and stacking on another.

The principle of compound interest can apply to all facets of life, not just the financial ones. And it can compound in your favor and against your favor.

Again, when I told Peter that I quit, he said, "Penny, I hired you to make decisions. What you do with the rest of your time is up to you."

Peter's coaching and the compounding of my problems remind me of the "80/20 rule," or the Pareto principle (referring to Vilfredo Pareto, who, in 1897, began successfully applying this ratio to economic systems). This principle says, essentially, that 80 percent of an event's outcomes (or outputs) are caused by 20 percent of its causes (or inputs). For my role, my actions and decisions were the 20 percent that produced 80 percent of the results. But I had been spending 80 percent of my time moving only 20 percent of the needle.

Let me give you two concrete examples. Ed Breen, who has twenty-three years of CEO experience (most notably at DuPont), famously said there were maybe fifteen decisions he made in all those years as CEO that really mattered. FIFTEEN. Sure, he made decisions daily, but the job of the CEO is to make those few value-creating, pivotal decisions when they arise. The effective CEO knows to focus on the key 20 percent.

Example two: After a decade away, Steve Jobs returned to

Apple, and its stock quickly rose more than 9,000 percent. The biggest change Jobs made to affect this turnaround? He focused. Apple had three hundred and fifty projects in development. Jobs whittled that down to fifty, and when that wasn't enough to get the Pareto principle spinning, he reduced Apple's projects down to ten. TEN from THREE HUNDRED AND FIFTY. The 20 percent, resulting in 9,000 percent growth.

This is the practical application of the Reset Mindset. By continually realigning and refocusing on what matters most—the 20 percent—you create a compounding effect. Just like Jobs went from three hundred and fifty to fifty to ten, I challenge you to run a decision through your Reset Mindset to identify the key 20 percent. And then, run that key 20 percent through again and identify the key 20 percent of *that* 20 percent. And so on, and so on. Because compounding doesn't just work inside you; it impacts everyone around you. Imagine your company with everyone focused on the tenth, or twentieth, or seven hundredth iteration of *their* 20 percent of 20 percent. It may sound like you're getting smaller, but in fact you are growing more and more effective. You are *multiplying* with every compounding practice.

The 80/20 rule, combined with the power of compounding, is a nuts-and-bolts way to imagine your Reset

Practice. As you do step three (Realign), ask yourself—pointedly—what is the 20 percent I need to realign toward?

As I've mentioned throughout this book, the impact of the Reset Mindset and its associated tools does not have to be limited to business and work. When you look for and then realign toward the 20 percent in other areas of your life—health, relationships, finances, spirituality, kindness—the same compounding, multiplying effect takes place. The growth in your life and humanity, just like at work, can be exponential. Not through effort, but through long-term impact. Simple and repeatable.

With each step taken, we actualize the compounding value and at the same time our focus on what we can control. Consider the following graphic as the value ladder for leadership using the three-step Reset Practice. Note how the steps within the practice build on each other and further compound with each Reset Moment. Awareness empowers your Adaptability, which leads to Alignment.

The Reset Practice is simple, repeatable, and compounding.

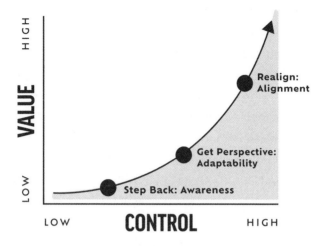

It's no accident that both the Value and Control axes increase as you continually realign. Remember our examples of Adrian and Leah? One of the categories of Reset Practices they invested in was Rules, like "No Work at Home" or "Get Up with Your Alarm." And the 80/20 rule is no different. What matters is the principle baked into the rule and how the rule supercharges your focus, your control, and the value of your choices. You can create and set whatever rules help you be more purposeful in your actions and interactions. You know what's effective for you. You know what you best respond to.

For example, General Colin Powell has a 70/40 rule.

He created this rule as a way to avoid making decisions too quickly and also to avoid "paralysis by analysis." He would refuse to make a decision until he had at least 40 percent of the necessary information, and similarly, he would refuse to hold off on deciding once he had 70 percent of the necessary information. At 70 percent, he's making a good choice!

There's nothing inherently magical about the numbers seventy and forty. General Powell set this framework up for himself because it fit his personality, emotional intelligence, and responsibilities. Rules act as a Reset Practice because they provide a structured framework to guide behavior and decision-making. As long as you structure them with intention, you can build whatever practices make sense in your life and workflow.

Quick Wins

Another super practical way to think about your Reset Practice is to focus on results from "Quick Wins."

United States Navy Admiral William H. McRaven famously said in a commencement address: "If you want to change the world, start off by making your bed." Admiral McRaven's advice is a perfect example of a Quick Win. By starting your day with a simple, quickly attainable task, you immediately gain a sense of accomplishment and even pride. And just like with compound interest, you'll then be eager to take on another task, and another.

Admiral McRaven added this deeper point: "Making your bed will also reinforce the fact that the little things in life matter. If you can't do the little things right, you'll never be able to do the big things right. And if by chance you have a miserable day, you will come home to a bed that is made—that you made. And a made bed gives you encouragement that tomorrow will be better."

Navy SEALs—some of the toughest people on the planet—are trained to make their beds first thing every day. There is an element of discipline to this as well, which is the same sort of discipline you need to take and make Reset Moments.

Reed Hastings, before he started Netflix, was a young engineer working late nights and drinking lots of coffee. He'd leave mugs scattered on his workstation, but the next day, he'd always find them cleaned and put away. Hastings assumed a cleaning crew must have been coming through. But one morning, he arrived extra early and found the CEO of the company washing his coffee mugs. The CEO said, "You do so much for us. It's the least I can do for you. I do it every morning when I come in." Imagine the impact that must have had on Hastings! How much loyalty and gratitude compounded from CEO to Reed to other workers. And what a significant Quick Win for that CEO each morning.

Quick Wins are a simple way to shift your focus from *effort* to *impact*. As a leader, using Quick Wins can build serious momentum, just like compound interest, specifically when you focus those Quick Wins on tasks and people that live in your 20 percent. You'll build morale and demonstrate daily progress.

Finding the Root Cause

Another benefit of the Reset Mindset is that you will be much more apt to identify the root causes of persistent problems. So often, in business and at home, we address merely the symptoms without taking the time to do the work required to uncover the true issue, because the presenting problem is not always the *real* problem. Symptoms may point us toward the truth, but if we correct the symptoms without engaging with the root cause, any relief will be only temporary.

A colleague recently expressed frustration to me about how her son brought home a report card filled with Ds. This child had a history of being a strong student, but upon reflection, my colleague realized that over the last several months, she had rarely seen him bringing textbooks home. At first, she wanted to punish her son, but she took the time to ask herself what other factors may be at play. What had changed? She spoke with her son, then with his teacher, and learned the school had moved almost all homework assignments online. Textbooks were being phased out. It wasn't that her son had suddenly become disinterested or distracted but simply that the logistics of homework had changed. After identifying this root cause, my colleague and her son adjusted his schedule and studying methodology, and within a few short weeks, those grades were turned around.

Taking a Reset Moment to ask questions helps identify the relationship between the real causes and the presenting problem. Even if it starts to feel redundant, remember that every time you take a step back, your perspective is increased.

Toyota made famous the Five Whys Method to get to the root cause: you simply ask and answer the question *Why?* five times. Each time we ask *Why?*, we force the

Every time you take a step back, your perspective is increased.

conversation away from the presenting problem and dig deeper. With each iteration, we gain relative perspective on the presenting problem to find the root cause. That is an example of the power of perspective-taking.

So if one of your team members suddenly starts missing deadlines, or meetings are running longer without being effective, don't simply react. Respond by identifying the root cause. Then you can dig it out and rid yourself of the true problem permanently. Keep resetting until you get there.

Early Detection System

On April 14, 1912, the Sunday after the *Titanic* sailed from Southampton, England, on its maiden voyage, Captain Edward J. Smith went about his normal Sunday routine, inspecting the ship. But instead of conducting the scheduled safety drill, he led a worship service. He then met with his officers to adjust the ship's course and speed. They continued at full speed, twenty-two knots. When the sun set, the temperatures dropped to freezing and turned the ocean's surface glassy, making it incredibly difficult for the crew to spot icebergs. Captain Smith, however, kept the ship at full speed, believing the crew could react in time if any icebergs were spotted. Unfortunately, as we all know, Captain Smith was wrong. The early detection systems put in place were either ignored or missed entirely. The ice field warnings that came in over the wireless? Ignored for having the wrong prefix and deprioritized in favor of passenger messages to shore. The binoculars that typically would have been in the hands of the lookout? Locked up in a storage container because no one thought to bring a spare when the officer with the key was bumped from the voyage.

The significance of paying attention to warning indicators cannot be overemphasized, because doing so can mean the difference between success and failure (and in the doomed *Titanic*'s case, life and death). Today's leaders are saying they don't have the time to lead. Canceling one-on-one meetings, overemphasizing numbers, a lack of account-ability from the team, and adding more activity rather than simplifying is equivalent to missing the safety checks. Reset Moments are those safety checks. Referring again to Paul O'Neill, his clear focus and alignment around safety empowered everyone to play a part in early detection. By creating space to dynamically evaluate circumstances, we can keep our awareness high and act swiftly to avert potential losses.

Even with the best early detection, mistakes will happen. They are inevitable. But again, being more intentional with your leadership prevents throwing good money after bad. Taking a purposeful pause to learn and adapt after a mistake enables you to turn it around sooner rather than letting it play out or snowball.

Early detection is always better than late reaction.

Reframe Your Thinking

Reframing is a technique that involves cognitive restructuring, replacing irrational thoughts with positive ones, and impacting our perception and interpretation of reality. Cognitive Behavioral Therapy (CBT) is built on this science. By acknowledging cognitive biases, reframing helps us see beyond our distorted perceptions, aiding in emotional regulation. This change in perspective enhances problem-solving by revealing new solutions and improves communication and conflict resolution by fostering understanding and de-escalating disputes.

And when reframing becomes instinctive—automatically transforming how you perceive and respond to situations? Well. That's evidence that your Reset Mindset is taking hold.

Reframing has far greater power than you may initially realize. Our emotional and behavioral responses shape our perceptions and interpretations of the world and people around us. So by altering our interpretation of a particular event, we can *intentionally* alter our feelings and actions.

As one of my colleagues is fond of saying: "Don't believe everything you think."

My first significant experience of reframing was after my father died. You'll recall I dug deeper with my questions, from *Why?* to *What does this mean?* to *What* else *can this mean?* That was my initial process for reframing my experience in order to direct my outcome.

Also, you'll recall that during my divorce, I had to grapple with the fact that my ex-husband was both a liar *and* a mentor. Both were true, and both were available to me as a way of thinking each day. By reframing the situation from "this man meant malicious intent" to "this was not meant to be personal, even though it feels personal," I could avoid several negative interpretations that helped avoid hurtful outcomes. I didn't drown in victimhood. I didn't let anger make co-parenting impossible. I could even find moments of grace and gratitude. By reframing the situation, I could see myself as strong and resilient rather than weak and broken.

Same with my kids. If I focused on how this might ruin their lives, I was certain to do just that. A child psychologist helped me reframe my thinking. "Every parent is guaranteed to screw up their child," he said. "Just do as little damage as possible." This simple phrase gave me permission to let go of trying to be the perfect parent. His advice reminded me of the physician's oath, "Do no harm." You see how a simple phrase or cue can be a way to dynamically reframe the situation and get you into your Reset Mindset. Those words triggered me to change my perspective on motherhood and led me to concentrate on my responses to situations rather than the situations themselves.

Reframing can be used in the workplace, too, and in a formalized way. It becomes a leadership tool that helps you develop a culture of awareness and opportunity. There are three players: the giver, the receiver, and the witnesses.

The giver provides a safe space and offers the receiver a positive alternative to a currently held perception or interpretation. That could come in many forms such as a question, a suggestion, or an observation. The receiver has the toughest job, as they must do the hard work of transforming an assumption or thought, and that typically means stepping back from a strong emotion. This is why a safe space—and witnesses—are important to the process.

As for the witnesses, they are there not just to hold the space for the giver and receiver but also to learn from the transformation happening before them. There is something incredibly inspiring about seeing someone adjust their point of view and actively improve themselves. The witnesses will be galvanized to change their own assumptions and biases as well, once they see it can be done.

The first few times might be clunky, but just like introducing the language of "Let's take a Reset Moment," once this process is understood and woven into the DNA of the workplace, it'll become like breathing. Your team members won't resist these opportunities to reframe; they'll *crave* them. Because each reframe will relieve anxiety, lessen negativity, and lead to more positive outcomes.

And as you become more practiced at reframing, you'll find that you can even be the giver, the receiver, and the witness, all at once. You'll have the ability to give yourself the reframing alternative.

Progress Is Perfection

Perfection is a pointless struggle. Perfection, by its very definition, is impossible. Because perfection implies there is no more room for improvement, advancement, or growth. And if you're no longer growing, guess what? You become stagnant. Reframing perfection as progress, however, allows for ongoing, never-ending change, growth, and development.

The Japanese have a cool term for progress: *kaizen*. Kaizen means "change for better," and it is a concept and a philosophy that focuses on continuous improvement in all aspects of life, including business and personal development. It reminds me of the DC Comics superhero Shazam, who must only say his name to call upon the wisdom of Solomon, the strength of Hercules, the stamina of Atlas, the power of Zeus, the courage of Achilles, and the speed of Mercury.

Maybe kaizen doesn't give you all of those superpowers,

but when you hold this belief, you have the willingness to reinvent processes, systems, and behaviors to achieve better outcomes.

Simon Sinek's work also mirrors the idea of continuous improvement in his book *The Infinite Game*. Sinek eloquently captures the essence of enduring success in business and life: it is not about being the best; it's about being better than yesterday. Reset Mindset recognizes that progress is the ultimate goal. Reset Moments help us play the infinite game and engage infinite thinking by understanding there is no finish line. Reset Moments help us maximize our potential.

In high school, tennis was my pursuit of perfection. I played on the varsity team, and—as you might imagine—I am competitive. I spent hours doing drills, trying to perfect my forehand, backhand, and especially my serve. I would get so frustrated and angry when my serve went long, or I hit the net.

During a crucial match, the pressure was mounting, and my confidence was waning. I was starting to defeat myself. Between sets, Mrs. Andrews, my coach, came over to me and said, "Remember, tennis is a game of moments. Each point is a fresh start, a chance to reset."

Keeping this in mind, I went back invigorated. Between each point, I focused on the Reset: taking a deep breath, swirling my racket three times, and thinking to myself, *Just relax and play this point.* With each point, I saw an opportunity to start fresh and apply the lessons from each previous point. I began to focus less on the scoreboard and more on playing each point to the best of my ability.

**The game is won one point at a time.
Progress, not perfection.**

CONCLUSION

THERE'S ALWAYS A RESET

It's 1914. December. And a lab in New Jersey owned by Thomas Edison catches fire. The inferno grows to such a roaring blaze that the local firefighters give up and just wait for it to burn itself out. In some situations, that's all you can do. Surrender.

But that doesn't mean you can't reset. Edison, standing in the gathered crowd, watched a million dollars worth of his equipment, prototypes, and research go up in smoke (that would be $30 million in today's dollars). But he didn't swear or curse or weep—any of which would have been an appropriate and justifiable response. Instead, he calmly turned to his son and said, "Go get your mother and all her friends. They'll never see a fire like this again."

The next morning, while picking through the ashes, Edison declared, "There is great value in disaster. All our mistakes are burned up. Thank God we can start anew."

Talk about having a Reset Mindset!

We all have experienced loss, hardship, change, challenge, and uncertainty in our lives. What differentiates us is how we prepare for and respond to those challenging times.

In my life, I've started businesses and sold them. I've experienced bankruptcy. I've hired and fired workers and team members and been hired and fired myself. I've driven myself to the point of burning out and been driven to the point of almost quitting. I've had my leadership questioned and undermined. I've lost friends, mentors, and family members. And I've experienced other significant lows.

But I have given myself permission (every time) to reset and start again with the lessons I learned—some of which are collected in this book.

Your anxiety and overwhelm can be handled. Your goals can be met and surpassed. You can overcome distractions and own your focus. You can engage more effectively with your teams and employees. You can boost connection and collaboration. You can increase efficiency and creativity, collectively and individually. You can handle complexity by embracing simplicity . . . if you practice.

You can handle complexity by embracing simplicity . . . if you practice.

And it all starts with the Reset Moment. These tools shift you from reactive to proactive. They are motivators and guides. They are both a thinking process and a set of actions. They free you emotionally and strengthen you practically. They are so simple, yet in that simplicity, you will find depth and clarity.

Once you load your Reset Mindset, you won't have to worry about "staying focused on what matters most" or "being innovative" or "practicing self-assessment" or "taking ownership" or "removing barriers." Because once your Reset Mindset is in place, you will do all of those things instinctively, even automatically. Those actions will become like breathing. You won't have to force yourself to do them, because you won't be able to not do them. It doesn't matter how jumbled your Rubik's Cube may be. It's just a few simple steps, done over and over, to get unstuck, focus on what matters most, and reach your goal faster.

I offer this book with excitement because of the potential it has to redefine your life and leadership journey in ways you may never have imagined.

Now go build your Reset Mindset— one Reset Moment at a time.

THE RESET MINDSET AS A MENTAL MODEL

You'll recall that choosing the most meaningful correct answer is one of the most powerful tools available to us. And just like there are many potentially correct answers, there are many Mental Models to help us make better decisions.

Mental Models are frameworks or theories that help us understand how the world works. They are critical-thinking tools to shape our points of view, and as such, they impact not just how we think about a situation but also how we approach it.

You have likely come across many Mental Models about universal truths. For example, looking at the world through the model of *velocity* helps you understand that speed and direction both matter. *Reciprocity* helps you understand that being positive and going first can make a big difference in how you are received and how others then react to you. And *margin of safety* is a Mental Model that helps you understand that things don't always go as planned.

But the Reset Mindset is the ultimate Mental Model because the practice can be applied to any situation. The Reset Mindset predisposes you to approach a challenge with fresh eyes, to be open to whatever perspective-taking reveals. As you continually realign, you'll find that sometimes velocity is useful, while other times reciprocity is called for. And when things don't go as planned? Well, simply taking a Reset Moment guarantees you have a margin of safety built in.

Basically, if all the other Mental Models are tools, then the Reset Mindset is the chest you can store them all in.

Let me break down the three steps of the Reset Practice in terms of some commonly used Mental Models so you can see its simplicity, practicality, and impact once again. (See the bibliography for references.)

1. Step Back

This involves taking a pause in your decision-making process to ensure that you're not operating on autopilot. Take inventory of where you are, objectively. During this phase, you might:

- Apply **Hanlon's Razor** ("never attribute to malice that which can be explained by stupidity") to avoid jumping to conclusions about others' intentions.
- Recognize the **Sunk-Cost Fallacy** to avoid continuing on a path just because you've already invested in it.
- Review **SWOT** analysis to help a person or organization identify Strengths, Weaknesses, Opportunities, and Threats related to business competition or project planning.
- Use the **Five Whys** to get to the root cause of a problem and ensure the team aligns around the problem to work collaboratively toward the solution.
- Choose the opposite with **Inversion Thinking**. Challenge your current perspective by selecting the opposite. It helps in identifying potential problems and avoiding blind spots in decision-making.

2. Get Perspective

This step is about widening your viewpoint to consider more information or different angles. It might involve:

- Using the **Pareto Principle (the 80/20 rule)** to identify which factors are the most influential in your current situation.
- Exploring **Cartesian Coordinates.** Used in NLP, this tool aids in viewing a situation from multiple dimensions by asking structured questions. It broadens understanding and facilitates a more comprehensive approach to problem-solving.
- Exploring *What else does this mean?* to challenge internal biases, groupthink, or limiting personal beliefs.
- Applying **Perceptual Positioning,** a simple role play to view a situation from different viewpoints, such as your own, another person's, and an observer's.
- Assessing the possibility of **Confirmation Bias** skewing your interpretation of the information.
- Asking *How might we?* or *How else?* to explore creative ideas for solving a problem.

3. Realign

Once you've taken a step back and gathered perspective, you then adjust your approach to better fit your objectives or values. This might mean:

- Using the **Theory of Constraints** to remove obstacles and barriers that limit capacity, growth, and engagement.
- Recognizing your **Circle of Competence** and either expanding it through learning or adapting your strategies to stay within it.
- Considering **Opportunity Cost** to make choices that better align with your goals.
- Embracing the **Gatekeepers Rule of 3** in blocking out distractions by predefining rules, adding support filters, and staging your environment to control and direct focus.

And that's just scratching the surface! In subsequent books, I will explore these frameworks and Mental Models more deeply and offer tools for specific applications such as employee engagement, sales and marketing, customer service, communication and conflict, innovation and problem-solving, and personal resilience.

YOUR RESET MOMENTS
SHARED WITH ME

What follows are a few testimonials from clients who offered to share their experiences working with these principles:

ERIN: I have been using Reset Practice for years. It started when I found out that my ten-year-old son was very ill. I had no time to feel sorry for myself or feel bad for him, and I needed to learn how to care for him. I took my sixty-second pity party and then focused on what I needed to do going forward. Now my whole family knows when something happens, you get sixty seconds of sorrow or doubt, and then it's time to shift your focus.

LYLA: I fall back on lines of scripture. When I am struggling with something, I find the line of scripture that brings me peace of mind, and everything seems a little easier after that. I never realized this was a Reset Practice; now I do it more consistently in all areas of my life.

JEFF: I was miserable at my job. The workload was not fairly distributed. I was asked to work through lunch and work nights and weekends . . . consistently. When I shared my concern with my boss, he brushed it off, and nothing changed. Over the next year, my attitude shifted and stress mounted. After reading Penny's LinkedIn posts about Reset Moments, I recognized a big one after the stress sent me to the cardiologist for a stress test. I took a Reset Moment and decided I had to set boundaries. When nothing changed, I left that job and feel so much better now. Why did I wait so long to take that Reset Moment?

BRIAN: Everyone was in panic around a decision that felt urgent because it involved the CEO. I brought up that this was a great time to reset. We all stood back and allowed ourselves to get some perspective on the matter and then realized that this was not as complicated as we thought—and it didn't need our immediate full-force response. What a relief!

BRANDON: We had the best sales this month that we have ever had in the history of the company. Instead of congratulating the team and moving on to push for the next BIG accomplishment, I stopped and asked the team to reflect on what specifically led to our success. We took thirty minutes to discuss this, so we were clear on what we needed to continue doing to maintain this level of success.

FAITH: I was working with several suppliers on a high-profile project. The delivery was due in my mailbox the night before, but it had not arrived. My personality is not to push or assert. I took a Reset Moment to call upon a different part of myself. I made it 100 percent clear this was unacceptable and irresponsible. No more excuses, it will [be] delivered by midnight tonight. The response—one word. Heard.

BRENDA: I was inspired by a conversation with a colleague and, as a result, prioritized my entire day to focus on tapping into a creative flow for writing my new book. I needed to go where my energy was. I'd been ignoring my plan to catch up on responding to emails, and this reset has paid off!

CHRIS: My Reset Practice is to take a Reset Moment every time I agree to take on something new. This makes me ask myself, "What do I have to say no to, in order to say yes to this?"

TELL ME ABOUT YOUR BEST RESET MOMENTS!

As you build your Reset Mindset, ask yourself:

1. *What experiences, revelations, and practices do you have to share?*

2. *In your interactions with others, how have you used Reset Moments?*

3. *What Reset Practices do you use that are successful for you, and what new Reset Practices have presented themselves?*

If you enjoyed this book, we would love to hear your thoughts, comments, ideas, and discoveries!

Please write them down on the next page and email them to me at **penny@pennyskeynote.com.**

I look forward to hearing about your journey!

BIBLIOGRAPHY

These references relate specifically to the concepts referenced in the "Afterword: The Reset Mindset as a Mental Model" section.

1. STEP BACK

Concept #1: Hanlon's Razor
Hanlon, R. "On the general applicability of the idea that political conflicts are misunderstandings." *Psychological Reports* 66, no. 3 (1990): 1039–1050. doi:10.2466/pr0.1990.66.3.1039.

Concept #2: Sunk-Cost Fallacy
Arkes, H. R. and C. Blumer, "The psychology of sunk cost." *Organizational Behavior and Human Decision Processes* 35, no. 1 (1985): 124–140. doi:10.1016/0749-5978(85)90049-4.

Concept #3: SWOT
Weihrich, H. "The TOWS matrix—A tool for situational analysis." *Long Range Planning* 15, no. 2 (1982): 54–66. doi:10.1016/0024-6301(82)90120-0.

Concept #4: Five Whys
Ohno, T. *Toyota Production System: Beyond Large-Scale Production.* CRC Press, 1988.

Concept #5: Inversion Thinking
Parrish, S. *Clear Thinking: Turning Ordinary Moments into Extraordinary Results* (New York: Portfolio, 2023).

2. GET PERSPECTIVE

Concept #1: The Pareto Principle

Koch, R. *The 80/20 Principle: The Secret to Achieving More with Less.* Crown Business, 1998.

Concepts #2-4: Cartesian Coordinates; What Else Does This Mean?; and Perceptual Positioning

Dilts, R., J. Grinder, R. Bandler, L. Cameron-Bandler, and J. DeLozier. *Neuro-Linguistic Programming Volume I.* Meta Publications, 1980.

Concept #5: Confirmation Bias

Nickerson, R. S. "Confirmation bias: A ubiquitous phenomenon in many guises." *Review of General Psychology* 2, no. 2 (1998): 175–220.

Concept #6: How Might We? or How Else?

Brown, T. "Design thinking." *Harvard Business Review* 86, no. 6 (2008): 84–89.

3. REALIGN

Concept #1: Theory of Constraints

Goldratt, E. M. and J. Cox. *The Goal: A Process of Ongoing Improvement.* North River Press, 2014.

Concept #2: Circle of Competence

Munger, C. T. "The Psychology of Human Misjudgment." Speech delivered at Harvard University. 1995.

Concept #3: Opportunity Cost

Mankiw, N. G. *Principles of Microeconomics* (6th ed.). Mason, OH: South-Western Cengage Learning, 2011.

Concept #4: Gatekeepers Rule of 3

Penny Zenker. *Accelerate Time Management Workbook* (2019): 34–35.

Penny Zenker. Gatekeepers Worksheet. 2020.

ACKNOWLEDGMENTS

I am so grateful for all who nurtured this message and brought it to life. I especially want to thank Jason Cannon and the diligent teams at Kevin Anderson and Amplify. Thanks also to my speaking audiences, who have deepened my work with their perspectives and applications.

Most of all, thanks to my loving family—my husband, Chuck; and my children, Sydney and Ethan—for putting up with me so focused on the book and inspiring me to be the best person, leader, and teacher I can be.

Last but not least, thanks to my mother, who modeled the Reset Mindset in her practices of broad forgiveness, always seeking solutions, and modeling resilience day after day, especially after my father died.

ABOUT THE AUTHOR

Penny Zenker (aka The Focusologist) is an international speaker, business strategy coach, and one of America's leading experts in the psychology of productivity to eliminate distraction, perfectionism, and self-sabotage to maximize results in every area of your life and business.

By the time she was thirty-one, Penny founded, developed, and sold her first multimillion-dollar business in Zurich, Switzerland. Later, she managed business unit turnarounds for a large market research company and served as a Tony Robbins business coach, helping entrepreneurs worldwide double their businesses.

Her first book, *The Productivity Zone*, was an instant Amazon bestseller, and her TEDx talk, "The Energy of Thought," has gained international attention and impact with more than one million views. Her engaging, inspiring, and interactive work teaches people to think and act more strategically and has been featured on NBC News, Forbes.com, ESPN, and Wharton Business Radio, among others.

Bonuses

Scan this QR code to access other videos, assessments, and worksheets to support your implementation of these concepts in your personal and professional life.

BONUSES

The Focusologist

Other Offers

Scan this QR code for more about my
first book, *The Productivity Zone*, which
introduces my high-performance framework
to help you get and stay in the zone.

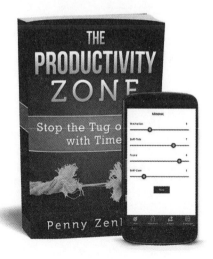